THE ART OF TORAH CANTILLATION

Ta-amei Hamikra · טַעֲמֵי הַמִּקְרָא

A STEP-BY-STEP GUIDE TO CHANTING TORAH

Cantor Marshall Portnoy

Cantor Josée Wolff

A Project of the Commission on Synagogue Music

Acknowledgments

We thank the following people for helping us bring this project to fruition:
Lynne Breslau, Susan Callen, Cantor Erik L. F. Contzius, Stephen Fontaine, Rabbi Daniel Freelander, Dr. Yossi Leshem, Kathy Parnass, Dr. Jane Portnoy, Cantor Judith Rowland, Gail Rudenstein, Dr. Eliyahu Schleifer, Rabbi David Straus, Dr. Judith Tischler, UAHC Press, Rabbi Max Weiss, and all of our colleagues and students who gave us invaluable feedback along the way.

Marshall Portnoy
Josée Wolff

THE ART OF TORAH CANTILLATION

Ta-amei Hamikra • טַעֲמֵי הַמִּקְרָא

Contents

Introduction		4
Lesson 1	Chanting a Phrase from Torah—The *Etnachta* Clause	5
Lesson 2	Ending a Verse of Torah—The *Sof-Pasuk* Clause	14
Lesson 3	How Cantillation Works	19
Lesson 4	The *Katon* Clause	22
Lesson 5	A Look at *Kadma*	31
Lesson 6	*Zakef Gadol*	36
Lesson 7	The *T'vir* Clause	37
Lesson 8	The *R'vi-i* Clause—Part One	43
Lesson 9	The *R'vi-i* Clause—Part Two	48
Lesson 10	*T'lisha K'tanah, Pazer, T'lisha G'dolah*	52
Lesson 11	The *Segol* Clause	58
Lesson 12	*Karnei Parah, Yare-ach Ben Yomo*	63
Lesson 13	You Can Chant Torah!	65
Appendix A	"Cantillation": A Historical Overview	68
Appendix B	Trope Relationships	71
Appendix C	Unusual Torah Portions	76
Appendix D	*Parashot*—Torah Portions	82
Appendix E	High Holy Day Cantillation	86
Appendix F	Scanning the *Tikkun*	87
Appendix G	Glossary of Terms Related to the Ritual of Reading Torah	89
Appendix H	Music Charts	92
Bibliography		96

Introduction

We are coming home to Torah because it is the very essence of our being and because we see as our first duty and greatest joy the teaching of those sacred texts that bind us to a shared faith and a shared way of life.

—Rabbi Eric H. Yoffie, President, UAHC

The chanting of Torah has always been the first and foremost way of transmitting our tradition. Knowledge of the trope or cantillation system is crucial not only to the understanding of our sacred text but also to its correct pronunciation and phrasing. It is our goal to train more and more members of our communities to become capable Torah readers and trope teachers. In the future, we hope that every UAHC congregation will have at least one Torah reader among its members.

To reach this goal, the Joint Commission on Synagogue Music has developed *The Art of Torah Cantillation*: טַעֲמֵי הַמִּקְרָא. These materials are intended for use by any student who possesses a basic level of Hebrew-reading fluency and is interested in learning how to chant, as well as by teachers who wish to fine-tune their cantillation skills.

The trope taught in this curriculum and presented on the accompanying CD is the version taught at Hebrew Union College-Jewish Institute of Religion, School of Sacred Music in New York. It is based on the musical notations of A. W. Binder and Cantor Lawrence Avery. This is the most commonly used trope in Reform congregations throughout North America.

All of the examples and exercises in the book are recorded on the accompanying CD. The numbers printed next to each exercise correspond to the track or ID numbers on the CD. Students are encouraged to use the recording first to learn the melodies of the trope patterns and second to compare their own chanting of the exercises to that of the teachers featured on the CD.

Ben Bag Bag used to say about Torah: "Turn it, and turn it, for everything is in it." (*Pirkei Avot* 5:22) May טַעֲמֵי הַמִּקְרָא provide you with yet another avenue to find more meaning in our sacred text so that you may be inspired to continue on the lifelong journey of תַּלְמוּד תּוֹרָה, the study of Torah.

Cantor Josée Wolff
Commission on Synagogue Music
New York, Kislev 5760/November 1999

LESSON 1

CHANTING A PHRASE FROM TORAH

The *Etnachta* Clause • מַעֲרֶכֶת אֶתְנַחְתָּא

Welcome to *The Art of Torah Cantillation*: טַעֲמֵי הַמִּקְרָא. The Torah is our sacred text. As such, we want to read it with the utmost respect and the greatest attention to detail. The art of chanting the Torah text dates back more than two thousand years and is described in the Talmud and numerous other sources. It is this ancient skill of chanting and thus interpreting the sacred text that this book sets out to teach.[1]

When you read any text out loud, what should you do to insure that you are understood? Of course, you must speak clearly and audibly. But there are also other tools that you use in reading aloud—tools you use so naturally that you may be unaware of them.

- First, you pause at the appropriate times.

Your voice inserts the commas and periods that help make the words understood. If you pause at the wrong time, you may convey a different meaning from the one the writer intended. For example, consider the following words:

WE DISLIKE FOOLISH PEOPLE LIKE YOU WE FIND THEM BORING

One way to read them is:
> *We dislike foolish people. Like you, we find them boring.*

Another possibility is:
> *We dislike foolish people like you. We find them boring.*

Without the use of punctuation, an author's intended meaning may be unclear.

---

[1] For a more detailed historical overview, see appendix A.

ﬡ � ﬗ ﬘

• Then there is the issue of stress.

How do you know whether to say **PRO**-ject or pro-**JECT**, בָּ֣נוּ (ba-**nu**: they built) or בָּ֣נוּ (**ba**-nu: us)? Context clues may help, but it's necessary to be very accurate when you read Torah. Guessing isn't good enough. This is where the cantillation symbols are extremely helpful: They indicate the correct placement of the accent.

• Furthermore, the cantillation you are about to learn adds a pleasant melody to the words. This melody is a nice "extra" because it helps us remember the text (Did you ever try to say "The Star-Spangled Banner"?) and makes the text much more enjoyable to hear.

The biblical cantillation system consists of twenty-eight symbols that tell you exactly how to punctuate the verses, on which syllable to stress each word, and how to chant each word or phrase. The Hebrew term for the cantillation symbols is טַעֲמֵי הַמִּקְרָא (*ta-amei hamikra*). The Hebrew word טַעַם means "taste" as well as "sense." The cantillation symbols literally help us make sense out of the text and give it its special "flavor." The symbols generally appear as part of a set pattern or phrase. We use the term "clause" or in Hebrew מַעֲרֶכֶת (*ma-arechet*) for each of those phrases.

There is some natural confusion about the term "to read" Torah because in reality, we do not usually read Torah but rather chant Torah. This is because the word "read" is one translation of the original Hebrew word קוֹרֵא (*koreh*). But קוֹרֵא also means "to call" or "to call out," which is much closer to the intended meaning in this context. Nevertheless, we continue to use the term "to read Torah" or "Torah reader," understanding that what we really mean is "to chant Torah" or "Torah chanter." Incidentally, the Hebrew term for a reading from Torah is קְרִיאָה (*k'ree-ah*). A male reader is a בַּעַל קוֹרֵא (*ba-al koreh*) or בַּעַל קְרִיאָה (*ba-al k'ree-ah*), and a female reader is a בַּעֲלַת קוֹרֵא (*ba-alat koreh*) or בַּעֲלַת קְרִיאָה (*ba-alat k'ree-ah*).

Here's how the system works. Each sign or symbol stands for a musical pattern. For example, this symbol written beneath a word stands for the following musical pattern:

ﬗ

This symbol is called מֵרְכָא (*mercha*), and it is chanted like this:

מֵרְכָא

Now let's apply מֵרְכָא to a word. Just for fun, let's put it beneath the English word "hello."

Can you chant the word? You should have chanted it like this: hello.

מֵרְכָא is one of the symbols that are used in cantillation. The symbols may look like curves, little lines, dots, or squiggles. Some appear beneath the word; others, above it. In cantillation we call such a symbol a trope. Some people use the word "trope" for the entire study of cantillation.

You have just learned the trope מֵרְכָא. Now try using it with a familiar Hebrew word. The word אֲשֶׁר means "which." How would you chant it with מֵרְכָא?

 אֲשֶׁר

You may have noticed something interesting about the trope. Not only is it notated beneath the word, it also appears beneath the very part of the word that should be stressed:

hello, אֲשֶׁר.

Therefore, one of the most important things cantillation does is indicate which syllable in a word should be stressed. The placement of the trope tells us not to say **HEL**lo but hel**LO**, not **A**-sher but a-**SHER**.

With a few exceptions, the trope is notated above or below the first letter of the stressed syllable, to the left of the vowel.

Here are a few examples from Torah with the trope מֵרְכָא. To practice, read the Hebrew word first, then sing the trope, and finally chant the words.

מֵרְכָא

אֲשֶׁר

לִהְיֹות

הָיְתָה

וּבֵין

You probably have noticed that the words you just practiced fit the melody of מֵרְכָא exactly because they all have the same number of syllables. When the actual word in a Torah text has more (or fewer) syllables than the name of the trope, you have to be flexible with the melody. For the following words, sing the first note of מֵרְכָא as many times as you need to until you reach the accented syllable (where the trope is):

וַיְדַבֵּר

עַל־מְזֻזֹות

בְּכָל־לְבָבְךָ

וְהָיוּ

וִהְיִיתֶם

In the next two examples, stay on the last note of מֵרְכָא to sing the last syllable:

וַיְהִי־עֶרֶב

וַיֹּאמֶר

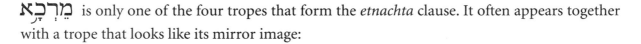

מֵרְכָא is only one of the four tropes that form the *etnachta* clause. It often appears together with a trope that looks like its mirror image:

This trope is called טִפְחָא (*tipcha*) and sounds like this: טִפְחָא

Together the two tropes sound like this: מֵרְכָא טִפְחָא

Now chant this combination in a few different ways. Try each example by chanting the tropes and then listen to the CD.

מֵרְכָא טִפְחָא

מֵרְכָא

טִפְחָא

טִפְחָא מֵרְכָא

מֵרְכָא טִפְחָא

One of the things that makes this combination easy is that טִפְחָא, the second trope, begins on the same note on which מֵרְכָא ends. Listen:

מֵרְכָא (note-same-the-on-stay) טִפְחָא

This connection makes things much easier! Whenever two tropes are related in this way, the arrows will remind you.

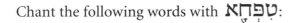

Chant the following words with טִפְחָא:

טִפְחָא

לְאֹות

הַיֹּום

בֵּיתֶךָ

In the examples below, chant the tropes first with their names and then chant the actual words. Listen to the recording as often as you like to hear each phrase chanted correctly–first the tropes, then the words.

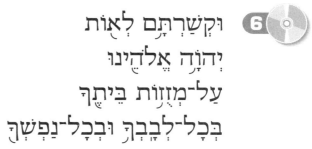

וּקְשַׁרְתֶּם לְאֹות

יְהֹוָה אֱלֹהֵינוּ

עַל־מְזֻזֹות בֵּיתֶךָ

בְּכָל־לְבָבְךָ וּבְכָל־נַפְשְׁךָ

You probably recognize the words you have just chanted. They are from the וְאָהַבְתָּ (*V'ahavta*) section of the שְׁמַע (*Sh'ma*). The text is found in the fifth and final book of the Torah, the Book of Deuteronomy, chapter 6, verses 4-9. The following examples are also from the *Sh'ma*. Chant the tropes, then the words, and finally listen to the tape.

הַיֹּום

וּבְשָׁכְבְּךָ

שְׁמַע

יְהֹוָה אֱלֹהֵינוּ

בְּכָל־לְבָבְךָ וּבְכָל־נַפְשְׁךָ

וְדִבַּרְתָּ

וּקְשַׁרְתֶּם לְאֹות

עַל־מְזֻזֹות בֵּיתֶךָ

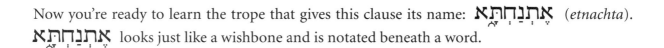

Now you're ready to learn the trope that gives this clause its name: אֶתְנַחְתָּא (etnachta).
אֶתְנַחְתָּא looks just like a wishbone and is notated beneath a word.

It sounds like this:

אֶתְנַחְתָּא

Try to sing it: אֶתְנַחְתָּא.

Now try a few words using אֶתְנַחְתָּא:

אֶתְנַחְתָּא

לֵאלֹהֶים

אֱלֹהֶיךָ

אֶת־כָּל־מִצְוֺתָי

עַל־יָדֶךָ

אֶתְנַחְתָּא functions as the main separator within a verse of Torah, very much like a comma
or semicolon. It divides the verse into two parts and is found in nearly every verse of Torah.
Practice the following phrases that end with אֶתְנַחְתָּא:

וּקְשַׁרְתֶּם לְאוֹת עַל־יָדֶךָ

לִהְיוֹת לָכֶם לֵאלֹהֶים

וַעֲשִׂיתֶם אֶת־כָּל־מִצְוֺתָי

שְׁמַע יִשְׂרָאֵל

וְדִבַּרְתָּ בָּם

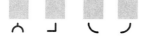
So far, you've learned אֶתְנַחְתָּא clauses of two and three words in the following two patterns:

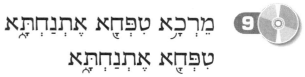

מֵרְכָא טִפְחָא אֶתְנַחְתָּא

טִפְחָא אֶתְנַחְתָּא

One additional trope completes the etnachta clause. This trope is called מֻנַּח (*munach*). It appears beneath a word and looks like a right angle:

מֻנַּח is a "servant" trope because it often comes before אֶתְנַחְתָּא and other separator tropes. מֻנַּח functions not as a separator but as a connector of words and phrases. Appearing before אֶתְנַחְתָּא, it sounds like this:

מֻנַּח

Here are some examples:

מֻנַּח אֶתְנַחְתָּא

בָּרָא אֱלֹהִים

יְהֹוָה אֱלֹהֶיךָ

וּמְאַת שָׁנָה

When מֻנַּח follows טִפְחָא, it begins on the same note on which טִפְחָא ends:

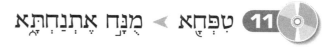

טִפְחָא ◄ מֻנַּח אֶתְנַחְתָּא

Here are the most common variations of the *etnachta* clause:

מֵרְכָא טִפְּחָא מֻנַּח אֶתְנַחְתָּא

טִפְּחָא מֻנַּח אֶתְנַחְתָּא

מֻנַּח אֶתְנַחְתָּא

מֵרְכָא טִפְּחָא אֶתְנַחְתָּא

טִפְּחָא אֶתְנַחְתָּא

You are now ready to practice some examples from Torah. It is helpful to follow these three steps:

1. Read the Hebrew words.
2. Chant the tropes, using their names.
3. Chant the text.

בְּרֵאשִׁית בָּרָא אֱלֹהִים

In the beginning God created,... (Gen. 1:1)

וַיֹּאמֶר אֱלֹהִים יְהִי־אוֹר

And God said, "Let there be light,..." (Gen. 1:3)

אֶת־הָאוֹר כִּי־טוֹב

...that the light was good,... (Gen. 1:4)

לֹא־תִשְׂנָא אֶת־אָחִיךָ בִּלְבָבֶךָ

You shall not hate your brother in your heart. (Lev. 19:17)

אֵת יְהֹוָה אֱלֹהֶיךָ

...*Adonai* your God,... (Deut. 6:5)

ENDING A VERSE OF TORAH

The *Sof-Pasuk* Clause • מַעֲרֶכֶת סוֹף־פָּסוּק

Before you learn more trope, this might be a good time to step back and look at the Torah as a whole. The Torah is divided into five books—Genesis, Exodus, Leviticus, Numbers, and Deuteronomy. Each book of the Torah is divided into a number of chapters and each chapter into a number of verses. For example, Genesis consists of fifty chapters, and the first chapter contains thirty-one verses. The names of the five books in Hebrew are:

(Genesis)	בְּרֵאשִׁית
(Exodus)	שְׁמוֹת
(Leviticus)	וַיִּקְרָא
(Numbers)	בְּמִדְבָּר
(Deuteronomy)	דְּבָרִים

Two other useful words are the Hebrew word for "chapter," which is פֶּרֶק (*perek*), and the Hebrew word for "verse," which is פָּסוּק (*pasuk*).[2]

If you want to refer to a particular chapter and verse of Torah, it is customary to insert a colon between the chapter and the verse. For example, the final verse of the Book of Genesis is notated as Genesis 50:26. If more than one chapter or verse is cited, we use a dash. Thus Gen. 50:23-26 means the Book of Genesis, chapter 50, verses 23 through 26, and Exod. 2:17-3:3 means the Book of Exodus, chapter 2, verse 17, through chapter 3, verse 3.

As was noted earlier, the most important purpose of cantillation is to indicate where to pause when reading the words of Torah so that the intended meaning of the text is clear. The most significant pause in any פָּסוּק of Torah is, of course, its concluding word, just as the most significant pause in any sentence is its final word. In English, that pause is denoted by a period that follows the final word.

---

2 For a glossary, see appendix F.

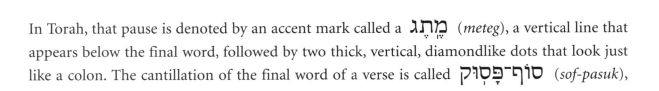

In Torah, that pause is denoted by an accent mark called a מֶתֶג (*meteg*), a vertical line that appears below the final word, followed by two thick, vertical, diamondlike dots that look just like a colon. The cantillation of the final word of a verse is called סוֹף־פָּסוּק (*sof-pasuk*), literally, "end of verse."

Here are some examples of *sof-pasuk*:

סוֹף־פָּסוּק:

וּבְקוּמֶךָ:

עַל־לְבָבֶךָ:

וּבִשְׁעָרֶיךָ:

וּבְכָל־מְאֹדֶךָ:

Only when both the colon and the accent mark are present do we
encounter the concluding word of a פָּסוּק.

A vertical line notated under a word and *not* followed by a colon is simply a מֶתֶג, an accent mark indicating secondary accents in the word. It has no melody associated with it. If you see a vertical line under a word and you are not sure what it is, always look for a colon. If a colon follows the word, you need to chant סוֹף־פָּסוּק:. If there is no colon, you don't have to worry about melody; just make sure you stress the indicated syllable!

To אֶתְנַחְתָּא, מֶנָּח, טִפְּחָא, מֶרְכָּא, and, we now add a fifth trope: סוֹף־פָּסוּק, which gives the *sof-pasuk* clause its name.

Here are some variations of the *etnachta* and *sof-pasuk* clauses that include all the tropes you
have learned so far. As you will notice, these two clauses have two tropes in common, מֵרְכָא
and טִפְחָא.

מֵרְכָא טִפְחָא מֻנַח אֶתְנַחְתָּא

טִפְחָא מֻנַח אֶתְנַחְתָּא

מֻנַח אֶתְנַחְתָּא

מֵרְכָא טִפְחָא מֵרְכָא סוֹף־פָּסוּק:

טִפְחָא מֵרְכָא סוֹף־פָּסוּק:

טִפְחָא סוֹף־פָּסוּק:

מֵרְכָא טִפְחָא סוֹף־פָּסוּק:

מֵרְכָא סוֹף־פָּסוּק:

Now practice some סוֹף־פָּסוּק: phrases from Torah. It is helpful to chant the tropes first and
then chant the words. Listen to the examples as much as you need to in order to hear the
phrases chanted correctly.

הַיּוֹם עַל־לְבָבֶךָ:

וּבְשָׁכְבְּךָ וּבְקוּמֶךָ:

בְּכָל־לְבָבְךָ וּבְכָל־נַפְשְׁךָ וּבְכָל־מְאֹדֶךָ:

וְהָיוּ לְטֹטָפֹת בֵּין עֵינֶיךָ:

עַל־מְזֻזוֹת בֵּיתֶךָ וּבִשְׁעָרֶיךָ:

Once you know the סוֹף־פָּסוּק: clause, you can chant complete Torah verses. Below are some examples. On the recording you will hear the tropes chanted first and then the words.

17

וּקְשַׁרְתֶּם לְאוֹת עַל־יָדֶךָ וְהָיוּ לְטֹטָפֹת בֵּין עֵינֶיךָ:

And you shall bind them for a sign upon your hand, and they shall be as frontlets between your eyes. (Deut. 6:8)

שְׁמַע יִשְׂרָאֵל יְהוָה אֱלֹהֵינוּ יְהוָה| אֶחָד:

Hear, O Israel, *Adonai* is our God, *Adonai* is One. (Deut. 6:4)

בְּרֵאשִׁית בָּרָא אֱלֹהִים אֵת הַשָּׁמַיִם וְאֵת הָאָרֶץ:

In the beginning God created the heavens and the earth. (Gen. 1:1)

וַיֹּאמֶר אֱלֹהִים יְהִי־אוֹר וַיְהִי־אוֹר:

And God said, "Let there be light"; and there was light. (Gen. 1:3)

בְּצֶלֶם אֱלֹהִים בָּרָא אֹתוֹ זָכָר וּנְקֵבָה בָּרָא אֹתָם:

…in the image of *Elohim* God created him; male and female God created them. (Gen. 1:27)

When you reach the end of an עֲלִיָה (*aliyah*), the סוֹף־פָּסוּק: clause has a special melody. You may have heard it chanted in your synagogue when the congregation joins in at the end of an עֲלִיָה. Here is what it sounds like:

18

מֵרְכָא טִפְחָא מֵרְכָא סוֹף־פָּסוּק:

טִפְחָא מֵרְכָא סוֹף־פָּסוּק:

מֵרְכָא טִפְחָא סוֹף־פָּסוּק:

טִפְחָא סוֹף־פָּסוּק:

וְאַתֶּם פְּרוּ וּרְבוּ שִׁרְצוּ בָאָרֶץ וּרְבוּ־בָהּ:

And you, be fruitful and multiply; bring forth abundantly on the earth and multiply on it. (Gen. 9:7)

Congratulations! You are now ready to chant your first Torah portion.

The following text is found in בַּמִּדְבָּר, the Book of Numbers, 34:24-28, in the weekly portion titled מַסְעֵי, *Masey*. You will notice that the text appears in two different ways—once with vowels and trope signs ("vocalized") and once in the calligraphy of the Torah scroll itself, without any vowels or punctuation ("unvocalized").

First take a look at the vocalized version and read the words. On the recording you will hear each verse chanted, first the tropes and then the words. Pretend that the last verse is the end of your *aliyah* and use the special melody you have just learned.

וּלְמַטֵּה בְנֵי־אֶפְרַיִם נָשִׂיא קְמוּאֵל בֶּן־שִׁפְטָן: וּלְמַטֵּה
בְנֵי־זְבוּלֻן נָשִׂיא אֱלִיצָפָן בֶּן־פַּרְנָךְ: וּלְמַטֵּה בְנֵי־יִשָּׂשכָר
נָשִׂיא פַּלְטִיאֵל בֶּן־עַזָּן: וּלְמַטֵּה בְנֵי־אָשֵׁר נָשִׂיא אֲחִיהוּד
בֶּן־שְׁלֹמִי: וּלְמַטֵּה בְנֵי־נַפְתָּלִי נָשִׂיא פְּדַהְאֵל בֶּן־עַמִּיהוּד:

And the prince of the tribe of the sons of Ephraim, Kemuel the son of Shiphtan. And the prince of the tribe of the sons of Zebulun, Elizaphan the son of Parnach. And the prince of the tribe of the sons of Issachar, Paltiel the son of Azzan. And the prince of the tribe of the sons of Asher, Ahihud the son of Shelomi. And the prince of the tribe of the sons of Naphtali, Pedahel the son of Ammihud. (Num. 34:24-28)

Once you have mastered all the tropes and chanted the phrases, you will be ready to attempt to read (= chant!) the text without seeing vowels or trope signs, just as it appears in the Torah scroll. Good luck!

ולמטה בני אפרים נשיא קמואל בן שפטן ולמטה
בני זבולן נשיא אליצפן בן פרנך ולמטה בני יששכר
נשיא פלטיאל בן עזן ולמטה בני אשר נשיא אחיהוד
בן שלמי ולמטה בני נפתלי נשיא פדהאל בן עמיהוד

HOW CANTILLATION WORKS

You have mastered two clauses in our system of Torah reading—the *etnachta* clause and the *sof-pasuk* clause. The *etnachta* and those tropes that lead up to it bring a verse of the Torah to a significant but not final pause. The *sof-pasuk* and those tropes that lead up to it bring a verse of the Torah to an end, as in the following example:

In the beginning God created

the heavens and the earth. (Gen. 1:1)

בְּרֵאשִׁית בָּרָא אֱלֹהִים

אֵת הַשָּׁמַיִם וְאֵת הָאָרֶץ:

Thus the *etnachta* functions as the main divider of the sentence, sometimes like a comma, sometimes like a semicolon, whereas the *sof-pasuk* is definitely a period.

Besides these two separators, we need more ways to subdivide the sentences in the Torah appropriately—to indicate commas, dashes, and other points of inflection. Consequently you will learn four more clauses, making a total of six. Once you have mastered the six clauses—and you already know two—you will be able to read Torah.

The six trope clauses may be thought of as six families of tropes. Each family has a "head" trope, with which the clause will always end. Within each clause are other tropes with varying degrees of "pausal power." These tropes can be divided into two groups:

- The tropes that indicate a pause in the flow of the text are called separators or מַפְסִיקִים (*mafsikim*; singular: מַפְסִיק, *mafsik*), also known as disjunctives or lords.
- In contrast, some tropes have no pausal power at all but flow right into the next trope. We call these tropes connectors or מְחַבְּרִים (*m'chabrim*; singular: מְחַבֵּר, *m'chaber*). They are also known as conjunctives or servants.

The "head" trope is always the strongest *mafsik* (separator) in any clause and gives the clause its name. The rest of the clause may include both *mafsikim* and *m'chabrim*. When a *m'chaber* (connector) comes just before a *mafsik* (separator), it "serves" the *mafsik*.

Mafsikim, such as *etnachta* and *sof-pasuk,* function as separators between clauses. Their separating power is not equal: *Sof-pasuk* is stronger than *etnachta,* and *etnachta* in turn is stronger than *tipcha.*

Take another look at the first verse of the Torah:

בְּרֵאשִׁית בָּרָא אֱלֹהִים
אֵת הַשָּׁמַיִם וְאֵת הָאָרֶץ:

This verse contains two clauses: an *etnachta* clause ending with the word *Elohim,* and a *sof-pasuk* clause ending with the word *ha-aretz.* The first clause contains three words with three tropes. The first trope, *tipcha,* is considered a *mafsik* with moderate pausal power. The second trope, *munach,* is a *m'chaber,* which flows directly into the third trope, *etnachta.* The second clause contains four words with four tropes. The first trope, *mercha,* is a *m'chaber* and flows directly into the *mafsik, tipcha.* Then follows another *mercha* serving the *sof-pasuk* on the last word.

If the verse were notated in English, it might look like this:

> In the beginning,   created God,   the heavens,   and the earth.

When you chant it, you make a slight pause after בְּרֵאשִׁית, a longer pause after אֱלֹהִים, and a clear stop after the final word of the verse, הָאָרֶץ:. The second and fourth words should flow without a pause into the next words, which they serve.

Here is a review of all the possible combinations in the two trope clauses we've learned so far:

Etnachta Clause מַעֲרֶכֶת אֶתְנַחְתָּא

אֶתְנַחְתָּא מִנַּח טִפְּחָא מֵרְכָא

אֶתְנַחְתָּא מִנַּח טִפְּחָא

אֶתְנַחְתָּא מִנַּח

אֶתְנַחְתָּא טִפְּחָא מֵרְכָא

אֶתְנַחְתָּא טִפְּחָא

אֶתְנַחְתָּא

Sof-Pasuk Clause מַעֲרֶכֶת סוֹף־פָּסוּק

סוֹף־פָּסוּק מֵרְכָא טִפְּחָא מֵרְכָא

סוֹף־פָּסוּק מֵרְכָא טִפְּחָא

סוֹף־פָּסוּק טִפְּחָא

סוֹף־פָּסוּק מֵרְכָא טִפְּחָא

סוֹף־פָּסוּק מֵרְכָא

סוֹף־פָּסוּק

LESSON 4

The *Katon* Clause • מַעֲרֶכֶת קָטֹן

The next trope clause concludes with קָטֹן (*katon*), two dots vertically arranged and placed over the first letter of a word's accented syllable:

You may hear it called *zakef katon*, *zakef katan*, or just *zakef*. Although all these terms are correct, in the following pages, we will use the term קָטֹן. When we hear the word קָטֹן, we are likely to think of the Hebrew word קָטָן, meaning small. Although the dots are small, they are powerful! קָטֹן is a מַפְסִיק (separator) that brings to a temporary halt an important phrase within a verse of Torah. Here are some examples:

אֲשֶׁר הוֹצֵאתִי אֶתְכֶם מֵאֶרֶץ מִצְרַיִם
לִהְיוֹת לָכֶם לֵאלֹהִים

…who led you out of the land of **Egypt**
to be your God,… (Num. 15:41)

בְּשִׁבְתְּךָ בְּבֵיתֶךָ וּבְלֶכְתְּךָ בַדֶּרֶךְ
וּבְשָׁכְבְּךָ וּבְקוּמֶךָ:

…when you sit in your house, and when you walk on **the road**
and when you lie down and when you rise up. (Deut. 6:7)

We chant קָטֹן like this:

The chant goes up and down, bringing the phrase to a temporary halt within the verse.

> Originally, long before tropes were written down, Torah readers were reminded of the melodies by hand signals. This method of music teaching is called cheironomy, a Greek term that means "teaching melody with one's hands." In some Jewish communities, this system is still being used. The more tropes you know, the more you realize that some got their shape from the hand signals.

Practice the following words with קָטֹן:

קָטֹן **21**

מִצְרַיִם

עַל־הָאָרֶץ

בַּדֶּרֶךְ

תִּזְכְּרוּ

An important "servant" or "helper" of קָטֹן—that is, a trope that leads us to it—is פַּשְׁטָא֙ (*pashta*).

This very common trope is the first of several that are always notated above the last letter of a word. These tropes are called "postpositive."

פַּשְׁטָא֙ (*pashta*) **appears above a word's final letter.**

It sounds almost the way it looks, starting low and jumping up, like this: פַּשְׁטָא֙. **22**

Practice the following words with פַּשְׁטָא֙:

לָאוֹר֙

אֲשֶׁר֙

אֶתְכֶם֙

לַיַּבָּשָׁה֙

The "over-the-last-letter" rule about פַּשְׁטָא֙ presents an interesting problem that you may have already anticipated. One of the fundamental purposes of cantillation is, of course, to indicate the accented syllable. If a פַּשְׁטָא֙ word is accented on the last syllable—like most Hebrew words—there is no problem. But what if a word is accented on a different syllable, like the word בְּבֵיתֶךָ or הַשָּׁמַיִם?

In that case, you will see the פַּשְׁטָא symbol twice:

Once over the final letter of the word, to indicate that it is indeed a פַּשְׁטָא, and once over the accented syllable, like this: בְּבֵיתֶךָ or הַשָּׁמַיִם.

Here are some examples. After you have tried to chant each word, listen to the recording to hear if you did it right.

לָאוֹר

הַדַּעַת

הַמַּיִם

וְאֶת־הַבְּהֵמָה

הַשָּׁמַיִם

וַיֹּאמֶר

Practice the following combinations of פַּשְׁטָא and קָטֹן:

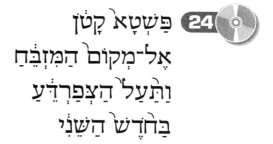

פַּשְׁטָא קָטֹן

אֶל־מְקוֹם הַמִּזְבֵּחַ

וַתַּעַל הַצְּפַרְדֵּעַ

בַּחֹדֶשׁ הַשֵּׁנִי

פַּשְׁטָא is often preceded by מַהְפָּךְ (mahpach). מַהְפָּךְ looks somewhat like the arithmetic sign for "less than" and is always notated beneath a word:

מַהְפָּךְ is a מְחַבֵּר (_m'chaber_) and functions as a connector, or servant, just like מֻנַּח.

It sounds like this:

מַהְפָּךְ **25**

Try the following examples:

מַהְפָּךְ

וַיַּרְא

וְהָיוּ

הוֹצֵאתִי

בֵּין

בְּשִׁבְתְּךָ

מַהְפָּךְ and פַּשְׁטָא enjoy such a close relationship that you will not be surprised to learn that פַּשְׁטָא begins on the same note on which מַהְפָּךְ ends, as in the case of מֵרְכָא and טִפְחָא:

מַהְפָּךְ ◄ פַּשְׁטָא **25**

הוֹצֵאתִי אֶתְכֶם

בְּשִׁבְתְּךָ בְּבֵיתֶךָ

בֵּין הַמַּיִם

וַיַּרְא אֱלֹהִים

וְהָיוּ לִמְאוֹרֹת

With מַהְפָּךְ – פַּשְׁטָא֙ – קָטֹן, you have almost mastered the *katon* clause. The following examples from the Torah include the tropes you have just learned, as well as a review of the earlier tropes.

מַהְפָּ֤ךְ פַּשְׁטָא֙ קָטֹן

וַיֹּ֥אמֶר לָבָ֖ן לְיַעֲקֹ֑ב

And Laban said to Jacob… (Gen. 31:26)

לָ֤מָּה נַחְבֵּ֙אתָ֙ לִבְרֹ֔חַ וַתִּגְנֹ֖ב אֹתִ֑י

Why did you flee away secretly and steal away from me,… (Gen. 31:27)

אֲשֶׁ֤ר בַּשָּׁמַ֙יִם֙ מִמַּ֔עַל וַאֲשֶׁ֥ר בָּאָ֖רֶץ מִתָּ֑חַת
וַאֲשֶׁ֥ר בַּמַּ֖יִם מִתַּ֥חַת לָאָ֑רֶץ׃

…of what is in the heavens above, or on the earth beneath, or in the waters under the earth. (Exod. 20:4)

שֵׁ֤שֶׁת יָמִים֙ תַּעֲבֹ֔ד וּבַיּ֥וֹם הַשְּׁבִיעִ֖י תִּשְׁבֹּ֑ת
בֶּחָרִ֥ישׁ וּבַקָּצִ֖יר תִּשְׁבֹּֽת׃

Six days you shall work, but on the seventh day you shall rest; even at plowing time and harvest time you shall rest. (Exod. 34:21)

You need to learn—or, more accurately, relearn—one more trope in order to complete your understanding of the *katon* clause. This trope is one that you already know—the one that is shaped like a right angle. It is the trope called מֻנַּח (*munach*). Although the word מֻנַּח comes from the root "to rest," this trope never rests! מֻנַּח is the ultimate connector or servant. It serves אֶתְנַחְתָּא, as we learned earlier. It also serves קָטֹן and other tropes.

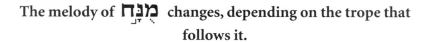

The melody of מֻנַּח changes, depending on the trope that
follows it.

Before קָטֹן, the melody of מֻנַּח is a little higher, leading into קָטֹן. Try to sing each phrase
below, and then listen and repeat each one:

מֻנַּח ‹ קָטֹן **28**

וְשִׁנַּנְתָּם לְבָנֶיךָ

וּבְלֶכְתְּךָ בַדֶּרֶךְ

מֵאֶרֶץ מִצְרָיִם

לְמַעַן תִּזְכְּרוּ

The following are the most common variations of מַעֲרֶכֶת קָטֹן, the *katon* clause:

מַהְפָּךְ ‹ פַּשְׁטָא ‹ מֻנַּח ‹ קָטֹן **29**

מַהְפָּךְ ‹ פַּשְׁטָא ‹ קָטֹן

פַּשְׁטָא ‹ מֻנַּח ‹ קָטֹן

מֻנַּח ‹ קָטֹן

פַּשְׁטָא ‹ קָטֹן

The following examples from Torah use all the tropes you have learned so far. As the examples
get longer, you will have to break down each one into its various clauses and practice it in the
following way:

Find the trope that gives each clause its name (e.g., *sof-pasuk, etnachta, katon*). Each of these
tropes marks the end of a clause. For each clause:

1. Read the Hebrew words.
2. Chant the tropes, using their names.
3. Chant the actual text.

When you have done the above, put all the clauses together and chant the entire example.

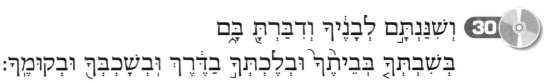

וְשִׁנַּנְתָּם לְבָנֶיךָ וְדִבַּרְתָּ בָּם
בְּשִׁבְתְּךָ בְּבֵיתֶךָ וּבְלֶכְתְּךָ בַדֶּרֶךְ וּבְשָׁכְבְּךָ וּבְקוּמֶךָ:

Impress them upon your children and talk of them when you sit in your house, and when you walk on the road, and when you lie down, and when you get up. (Deut. 6:7)

לְמַעַן תִּזְכְּרוּ וַעֲשִׂיתֶם אֶת־כָּל־מִצְוֹתָי
וִהְיִיתֶם קְדֹשִׁים לֵאלֹהֵיכֶם:

Thus you shall remember and do all My commandments, and be holy to your God. (Num. 15:40)

לֹא־תִקֹּם וְלֹא־תִטֹּר אֶת־בְּנֵי עַמֶּךָ
וְאָהַבְתָּ לְרֵעֲךָ כָּמוֹךָ אֲנִי יְהוָה:

You shall not avenge nor bear any grudge against the children of your people. You shall love your neighbor as yourself; I am *Adonai*. (Lev. 19:18)

וַיְכַל אֱלֹהִים בַּיּוֹם הַשְּׁבִיעִי מְלַאכְתּוֹ אֲשֶׁר עָשָׂה
וַיִּשְׁבֹּת בַּיּוֹם הַשְּׁבִיעִי מִכָּל־מְלַאכְתּוֹ אֲשֶׁר עָשָׂה:

And on the seventh day God ended the work that God had made, and God rested on the seventh day from all the work that God had made. (Gen. 2:2)

אֲשֶׁר בַּשָּׁמַיִם מִמַּעַל וַאֲשֶׁר בָּאָרֶץ מִתַּחַת
וַאֲשֶׁר בַּמַּיִם מִתַּחַת לָאָרֶץ:

…of what is in the heavens above, or on the earth beneath, or in the waters under the earth. (Exod. 20:4)

שֵׁשֶׁת יָמִים תַּעֲבֹד וְעָשִׂיתָ כָּל־מְלַאכְתֶּךָ:

Six days shall you labor and do all your work. (Exod. 20:9)

וְיוֹם הַשְּׁבִיעִי שַׁבָּת לַיהוָה אֱלֹהֶיךָ

But the seventh day is a Sabbath of *Adonai* your God,… (Exod. 20:10)

There is a trope that looks just like מַהְפָּךְ but is called יְתִיב (*y'tiv*).

Although יְתִיב may look like מַהְפָּךְ at first glance, its function and sound are very different. Here are some ways to tell the two tropes apart:

1. יְתִיב appears only when the first word of the clause is stressed on the first syllable.
2. It always appears underneath the first letter of the word *and a little to the right.*
3. It is always followed by קָטֹן or מְנַח קָטֹן (whereas מַהְפָּךְ is always followed by פַּשְׁטָא).

Here is how יְתִיב sounds:

יְתִיב

Try the following examples of *katon* clauses with the trope יְתִיב

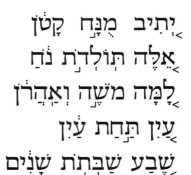

יְתִיב מְנַח קָטֹן
אֵלֶּה תּוֹלְדֹת נֹחַ
לָמָה משֶׁה וְאַהֲרֹן
עַיִן תַּחַת עַיִן
שֶׁבַע שַׁבְּתֹת שָׁנִים

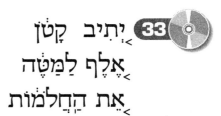

יְתִיב קָטֹן
אֶלֶף לַמַּטֶּה
אֶת הַחֲלֹמוֹת

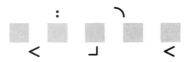
Now practice the following phrases that include *katon* clauses with the trope יְתִיב

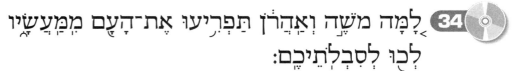

לָמָּה מֹשֶׁה וְאַהֲרֹן תַּפְרִיעוּ אֶת־הָעָם מִמַּעֲשָׂיו לְכוּ לְסִבְלֹתֵיכֶם:

Why do you, Moses and Aaron, take the people from their tasks? Get to your labors. (Exod. 5:4)

עַיִן תַּחַת עַיִן שֵׁן תַּחַת שֵׁן יָד תַּחַת יָד רֶגֶל תַּחַת רָגֶל:

…eye for eye, tooth for tooth, hand for hand, foot for foot. (Exod. 21:24)

שֶׁבַע שַׁבְּתֹת שָׁנִים שֶׁבַע שָׁנִים שֶׁבַע פְּעָמִים

You shall count off seven weeks of years, seven times seven years… (Lev. 25:8)

אֶלֶף לַמַּטֶּה אֶלֶף לַמַּטֶּה לְכֹל מַטּוֹת יִשְׂרָאֵל תִּשְׁלְחוּ לַצָּבָא:

From every tribe a thousand, throughout all the tribes of Israel, shall you send to the army. (Num. 31:4)

וַיִּזְכֹּר יוֹסֵף אֵת הַחֲלֹמוֹת אֲשֶׁר חָלַם לָהֶם

And Joseph remembered the dreams that he dreamed about them. (Gen. 42:9)

Congratulations! You have now mastered three of the six clauses in the cantillation of Torah and have learned ten tropes. These clauses and tropes cover about three-quarters of the Torah text.

A Look at *Kadma* • קַדְמָא

When you first look at the trope קַדְמָא (*kadma*), you may notice that it looks exactly like פַּשְׁטָא (*pashta*). Therefore, before you begin to use this trope, let's learn how to distinguish it from its twin. Although the two may look identical, they are fundamentally different in character and purpose.

The first difference is their placement on a word. You will recall that פַּשְׁטָא always appears above the final letter of a word. Therefore, if a trope that looks exactly like פַּשְׁטָא is notated above another letter, it is not a פַּשְׁטָא but a קַדְמָא. קַדְמָא, like most tropes, is notated above the first letter of a word's accented syllable.

For example: אֲשֶׁר (*kadma*)

אֲשֶׁר (*pashta*)

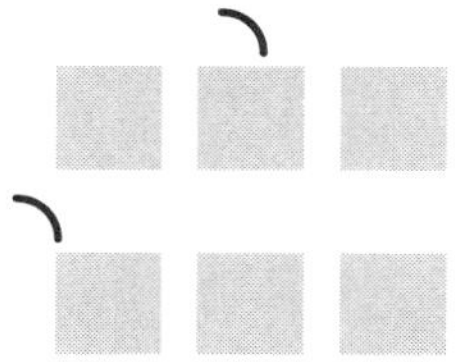

More important, however, is the contrast in the way the two tropes function. פַּשְׁטָא is a מַפְסִיק (separator), bringing a short phrase within a katon clause to a temporary pause, as in the following examples:

הוֹצֵאתִי אֶתְכֶם\ מֵאֶרֶץ מִצְרָיִם

I brought **you out** / from the land of Egypt… (Num. 15: 41)

יְהִי מְאֹרֹת\ בִּרְקִיעַ הַשָּׁמַיִם

Let there be **lights** / in the firmament of the heavens,… (Gen. 1:14)

קַדְמָא on the other hand, is a connector, leading us to the next word in the text:

וַיִּבְרָא אֱלֹהִים אֶת־הָאָדָם\ בְּצַלְמוֹ

And so created God the human / in God's image... (Gen.1:27)

וְשֵׁם הַנָּהָר הַשְּׁלִישִׁי\ חִדֶּקֶל

And the name of the third river / is Chidekel... (Gen. 2:14)

Be aware that like מֻנַּח, the melody of קַדְמָא may change, depending upon which trope follows it. You will recall that the melody of the trope מֻנַּח sounds one way when it appears before אֶתְנַחְתָּא and quite another way before קָטֹן. Our understanding of מֻנַּח and now קַדְמָא leads us to an important generalization about the melodic patterns of the tropes:

The melody of the מַפְסִיקִים (separators) is constant, while
the melody of some מְחַבְּרִים (connectors) varies, depending
upon which trope follows them.

When קַדְמָא serves מַהְפַּךְ, that is, when it immediately precedes מַהְפַּךְ, its melody has just two notes, the second higher than the first and leading right into מַהְפַּךְ:

קַדְמָא

קַדְמָא ◄ מַהְפַּךְ

Practice the following combinations from Torah:

אֲשֶׁר הוֹצֵאתִי

וַיִּסַּע מֹשֶׁה

וְגַם הֲקִמֹתִי

אֲשֶׁר־הָיָה לָךְ

Now for more of a challenge, practice some longer phrases from Torah that utilize all the tropes you have learned so far. Be sure to notice the difference between פַּשְׁטָא and קַדְמָא. It is helpful to chant the tropes alone first, and then chant the text.

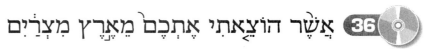

אֲשֶׁ֣ר הוֹצֵ֧אתִי אֶתְכֶם֙ מֵאֶ֣רֶץ מִצְרַ֔יִם

...who brought you out of the land of Egypt... (Num.15: 41)

וַיַּסַּ֨ע מֹשֶׁ֤ה אֶת־יִשְׂרָאֵל֙ מִיַּם־ס֔וּף וַיֵּצְא֖וּ אֶל־מִדְבַּר־שׁ֑וּר

So Moses brought Israel from the Red Sea, and they went out into the **wilderness of Shur...**
(Exod. 15:22)

וְגַ֨ם הֲקִמֹ֤תִי אֶת־בְּרִיתִי֙ אִתָּ֔ם לָתֵ֥ת לָהֶ֖ם אֶת־אֶ֥רֶץ כְּנָ֑עַן

And I also established My covenant with them, to give them the land of Canaan...
(Exod. 6:4)

פְּרִ֨י עֵ֤ץ הָדָר֙ כַּפֹּ֣ת תְּמָרִ֔ים וַעֲנַ֥ף עֵץ־עָבֹ֖ת וְעַרְבֵי־נָ֑חַל

...the boughs of *hadar* trees, branches of palm trees, boughs of thick **trees, and willows of**
the brook... (Lev. 23:40)

וַיִּצְמָ֨א שָׁ֤ם הָעָם֙ לַמַּ֔יִם וַיָּ֥לֶן הָעָ֖ם עַל־מֹשֶׁ֑ה

And the people thirsted there for water, and the people murmured against Moses...
(Exod. 17:3)

To review all the tropes you have learned so far, try the following short Torah portion, Genesis 32:4-7, from וַיִּשְׁלַח. First look at the "vocalized" version that has the vowels and tropes printed and then at the "unvocalized" text as it appears in the Torah scroll itself, without any punctuation.

Read the words and make sure that you are comfortable with the Hebrew text.

Next separate the words according to the trope clauses. The most important break in the first verse is, of course, the last word _Edom_, with the trope _sof-pasuk_. The next most important separator is the _etnachta_ on the word _achiv_. Finally the _katon_ on the word _l'fanav_ shows you that you have a verse with three distinct clauses:

וַיִּשְׁלַ֨ח יַעֲקֹ֤ב מַלְאָכִים֙ לְפָנָ֔יו

אֶל־עֵשָׂ֖ו אָחִ֑יו

אַ֥רְצָה שֵׂעִ֖יר שְׂדֵ֥ה אֱד֖וֹם׀

Now try to chant the tropes in each clause:

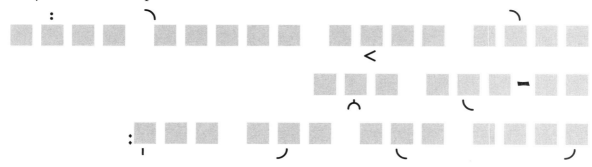

Finally chant the words, pausing slightly at _katon_ and _etnachta_ and a little more after _sof-pasuk_.

This four-step process will help you prepare your Torah reading step-by-step and will insure that you are comfortable with all aspects of the portion. The more you read Torah, the sooner you will go on "automatic pilot" and the basic reading and discerning of trope relationships will come instinctively. With practice, you will within a short time be able to "sight-read" a verse from Torah!

Now try the next few verses on your own. If you're feeling really adventuresome, chant the verses in the unvocalized calligraphy of the Torah scroll.

(37)

וַיִּשְׁלַ֨ח יַעֲקֹ֤ב מַלְאָכִים֙ לְפָנָ֔יו אֶל־עֵשָׂ֖ו אָחִ֑יו אַ֥רְצָה שֵׂעִ֖יר
שְׂדֵ֥ה אֱדֽוֹם: וַיְצַ֤ו אֹתָם֙ לֵאמֹ֔ר כֹּ֣ה תֹֽאמְר֔וּן לַֽאדֹנִ֖י לְעֵשָׂ֑ו
כֹּ֤ה אָמַר֙ עַבְדְּךָ֣ יַעֲקֹ֔ב עִם־לָבָ֣ן גַּ֔רְתִּי וָאֵחַ֖ר עַד־עָֽתָּה:
וַֽיְהִי־לִי֙ שׁ֣וֹר וַחֲמ֔וֹר צֹ֥אן וְעֶ֖בֶד וְשִׁפְחָ֑ה וָֽאֶשְׁלְחָה֙ לְהַגִּ֣יד
לַֽאדֹנִ֔י לִמְצֹא־חֵ֖ן בְּעֵינֶֽיךָ: וַיָּשֻׁ֙בוּ֙ הַמַּלְאָכִ֔ים אֶֽל־יַעֲקֹ֖ב
לֵאמֹ֑ר בָּ֤אנוּ אֶל־אָחִ֙יךָ֙ אֶל־עֵשָׂ֔ו וְגַם֙ הֹלֵ֣ךְ לִקְרָֽאתְךָ֔
וְאַרְבַּע־מֵא֥וֹת אִ֖ישׁ עִמּֽוֹ:

And Jacob sent messengers before him to Esau, his brother, in the land of Seir, the country of Edom. And he commanded them, saying, "Thus shall you speak to my lord Esau: Your servant Jacob said thus: I have sojourned with Laban and stayed there until now. And I have oxen, and asses, flocks, and menservants, and womenservants; and I have sent this message to my lord, in the hope that I may find favor in your sight." And the messengers returned to Jacob, saying, "We came to your brother, Esau, and also he comes to meet you, and four hundred men with him." (Gen. 32:4-7)

וישלח יעקב מלאכים לפניו אל עשו אחיו ארצה שעיר
שדה אדום ויצו אתם לאמר כה תאמרון לאדני לעשו
כה אמר עבדך יעקב עם לבן גרתי ואחר עד עתה
ויהי לי שור וחמור צאן ועבד ושפחה ואשלחה להגיד
לאדני למצא חן בעיניך וישבו המלאכים אל יעקב
לאמר באנו אל אחיך אל עשו וגם הלך לקראתך
וארבע מאות איש עמו

LESSON 6

Zakef-Gadol • זָקֵף גָּדוֹל

זָקֵף גָּדוֹל (*zakef gadol*) functions as a separator, just like קָטֹן ([*zakef*] *katon*). In fact, some consider it to be a substitute for a *katon* clause. It generally stands on its own and is easy to recognize: a vertical line flanked by two vertical dots on its right, above the first letter of a word's stressed syllable:

׀֗

Its sound is trumpetlike—three ascending notes followed by a descent that stops just a little higher than the opening tone:

זָקֵף גָּדֹול **38**

Practice this trope a number of times:

זָקֵף גָּדֹול
וַיְהִי־נֹחַ
לְהַבְדִּיל
לִשְׁמֹר

Chant the following phrases from the Torah that include זָקֵף גָּדֹול:

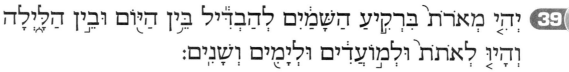 **39**

יְהִי מְאֹרֹת בִּרְקִיעַ הַשָּׁמַיִם לְהַבְדִּיל בֵּין הַיּוֹם וּבֵין הַלָּיְלָה
וְהָיוּ לְאֹתֹת וּלְמוֹעֲדִים וּלְיָמִים וְשָׁנִים:

Let there be lights in the firmament of the heavens to divide the day from the night; and let them serve as signs for seasons, and for days, and for years. (Gen. 1:14)

וְאֵת לַהַט הַחֶרֶב הַמִּתְהַפֶּכֶת לִשְׁמֹר אֶת־דֶּרֶךְ עֵץ הַחַיִּים:

…and a flaming sword that turned every way, to guard the way of the tree of life. (Gen. 3:24)

וַיְהִי־נֹחַ בֶּן־חֲמֵשׁ מֵאוֹת שָׁנָה
וַיּוֹלֶד נֹחַ אֶת־שֵׁם אֶת־חָם וְאֶת־יָפֶת:

And Noah was five hundred years old, and Noah fathered Shem, Ham, and Japheth. (Gen. 5:32)

The *T'vir* Clause • מַעֲרֶכֶת תְּבִיר

When you have heard Torah chanted in temple, you may have noticed that the Torah reader responds to the first Torah blessing with the word אָמֵן (amen).

The אָמֵן is chanted to a short melodic phrase that descends and then goes back up to the starting tone, like this:

 אָמֵן

This אָמֵן phrase is identical to the melody of the trope תְּבִיר:

 עַ

תְּבִיר is a *mafsik* (separator). It temporarily stops the thought within a verse, as in the following example:

וַיִּקְרָא הָאָדָם / שֵׁם אִשְׁתּוֹ חַוָּה / / כִּי / הִוא הָיְתָה אֵם כָּל־חָי:

And [thus] called *Adam* the name of his wife Eve, *because* she was the mother of all the living. (Gen. 3:20)

Here are some words that feature תְּבִיר:

תְּבִיר

אֹתָם

אָדָם

עָשָׂה־פְרִי

מְצַוְּךָ

Frequently תְּבִיר is preceded by a trope called דַּרְגָּא (*darga*). דַּרְגָּא is a *m'chaber* (a connector) that looks like a backward *z* (some editions of Torah use a backward *s*):

z

As you listen to דַּרְגָּא, you will note that דַּרְגָּא first goes up and then descends in short steps, like a scale:

דַּרְגָּא **41**

Try the following examples:

אֲשֶׁר

מִפְּרִי

אָנֹכִי

וַיְבָרֶךְ

וַיִּקְרָא

תְּבִיר starts on the same note on which דַּרְגָּא ends:

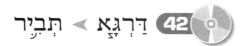

דַּרְגָּא ◄ תְּבִיר **42**

Practice the examples below:

אָנֹכִי מְצַוְּךָ

וַיְבָרֶךְ אֹתָם

וַיִּקְרָא אֱלֹהִים

מִפְּרִי הָאֲדָמָה

אֲשֶׁר צִוִּיתִךָ

תְּבִיר may also be preceded by מֵרְכָא, the same trope that preceded טִפְחָא. But מֵרְכָא, a connector, is chanted differently before תְּבִיר: It sounds like the first, second, and last note of דַּרְגָּא without the "in-between notes":

מֵרְכָא

Listen to and then chant each of the following examples:

תְּבִיר

מֵרְכָא ◄ תְּבִיר

דַּרְגָּא ◄ תְּבִיר

מֵרְכָא תְּבִיר

דַּרְגָּא תְּבִיר

Try the above again if you're not certain. When you're ready, chant the following examples from Torah:

וַיִּקְרָא הָאָדָם

וְהָיָה לְךָ

מֵעוֹף הַשָּׁמַיִם

וַיִּגְבְּרוּ הַמַּיִם

אֲשֶׁר צִוִּיתִיךָ

צַוֵּה אֹתוֹ

תִּקַּח־לָךְ

Either מֵנָח or קַדְמָא can be preceded by מֵרְכָא תְּבִיר or דַּרְגָּא תְּבִיר.

מַהְפַּךְ before קַדְמָא is exactly like קַדְמָא before מֵרְכָא תְּבִיר or דַּרְגָּא תְּבִיר. It also ends on the same note on which דַּרְגָּא and מֵרְכָא start.

Here are some combinations:

קַדְמָא ◄ דַּרְגָּא ◄ תְּבִיר

אֲשֶׁר אָנֹכִי מְצַוֶּךָ
לָתֵת תֶּבֶן לָעָם

קַדְמָא ◄ מֵרְכָא ◄ תְּבִיר

וְנָתַתִּי אֹתָהּ לָכֶם
זָבַת חָלָב וּדְבַשׁ

מֵנָח before מֵרְכָא תְּבִיר or דַּרְגָּא תְּבִיר begins high, jumps down, then goes back up.

Listen:

מֵנָח

Practice the following examples of the various combinations:

מֵנָח דַּרְגָּא תְּבִיר
דֶּגֶל מַחֲנֵה רְאוּבֵן

מֵנָח מֵרְכָא תְּבִיר
עַד אַרְבָּעָה עָשָׂר

When you are ready to chant some text, chant the following passages from Torah. Remember to follow the four-step process outlined in lesson 5.

47

וַיַּרְא אֱלֹהִים אֶת־הָאוֹר כִּי־טֶוֹב
וַיַּבְדֵּל אֱלֹהִים בֵּין הָאוֹר וּבֵין הַחֹשֶׁךְ:

And God saw that the light was good, and God separated the light from the darkness. (Gen. 1:4)

לָתֵת תֶּבֶן לָעָם לִלְבֹּן הַלְּבֵנִים כִּתְמוֹל שִׁלְשֹׁם

…[no longer] give the people straw to make bricks as till now,… (Exod. 5:7)

וְהָיָה לָכֶם לְמִשְׁמֶרֶת עַד אַרְבָּעָה עָשָׂר יוֹם לַחֹדֶשׁ הַזֶּה

And you shall watch over it until the fourteenth day of the same month. (Exod. 12:6)

וְלֹא־נוֹתַר כָּל־יֶרֶק בָּעֵץ וּבְעֵשֶׂב הַשָּׂדֶה בְּכָל־אֶרֶץ מִצְרָיִם:

…and there remained not any green thing in the trees or in the herbs of the field through all the land of Egypt. (Exod. 10:15)

דֶּגֶל מַחֲנֵה רְאוּבֵן תֵּימָנָה לְצִבְאֹתָם
וְנָשִׂיא לִבְנֵי רְאוּבֵן אֱלִיצוּר בֶּן־שְׁדֵיאוּר:

On the south side shall be the standard of the camp of Reuben according to their armies, and the captain of the sons of Reuben shall be Elizur the son of Shedeur. (Num. 2:10)

דֶּגֶל מַחֲנֵה אֶפְרַיִם לְצִבְאֹתָם יָמָּה
וְנָשִׂיא לִבְנֵי אֶפְרַיִם אֱלִישָׁמָע בֶּן־עַמִּיהוּד:

On the west side shall be the standard of the camp of Ephraim according to their armies, and the captain of the sons of Ephraim shall be Elishama the son of Ammihud. (Num. 2:18)

מֵרְכָא כְּפוּלָה

There are five occasions in Torah on which the trope מֵרְכָא כְּפוּלָה (*mercha k'fulah*) takes the place of *t'vir*. מֵרְכָא כְּפוּלָה ("double mercha") looks like two merchas, one nestled within the other:

It is chanted as a short four-note scale, starting on the last note of דַּרְגָּא, going up, then down:

מֵרְכָא כְּפוּלָה

It is always preceded by דַּרְגָּא and followed by טִפְחָא:

דַּרְגָּא ◄ מֵרְכָא כְּפוּלָה ◄ טִפְחָא

Chant each of the following five examples:

וַיַּגֶּשׁ־לוֹ וַיֹּאכַל וַיָּבֵא לוֹ יַיִן וַיֵּשְׁתְּ:

…and he brought it near to him and he ate, and he brought him wine and he drank. (Gen. 27:25)

לָמָה תַעֲשֶׂה כֹה לַעֲבָדֶיךָ:

…"why do you deal thus with your servants?" (Exod. 5:15)

לִפְנֵי יְהֹוָה אֵשׁ זָרָה אֲשֶׁר לֹא צִוָּה אֹתָם:

…a strange fire before God, which God commanded them not. (Lev. 10:1)

הֲלוֹא טוֹב לָנוּ שׁוּב מִצְרָיְמָה:

"Would it not be better for us to return to Egypt?" (Num. 14:3)

וְנֹבַח הָלַךְ וַיִּלְכֹּד אֶת־קְנָת וְאֶת־בְּנֹתֶיהָ וַיִּקְרָא לָהּ נֹבַח בִּשְׁמוֹ:

And Nobah went and captured Kenath and its villages and called it Nobah, after his own name. (Num. 32:42)

LESSON 8

The *R'vi-i* Clause • מַעֲרֶכֶת רְבִיעִי

Part One

The Hebrew word רְבִיעִי (*r'vi-i*) means "fourth" (from the word אַרְבַּע, "four") and the diamond-shaped trope רְבִיעִי has four sides:

רְבִיעִי is a separator and sounds like this:

רְבִיעִי

Chant the following words with רְבִיעִי:

שְׁקָלִים
הַשָּׁנִים
הַשְּׁלִישִׁי
הָאֵלֶּה

NOTE: In some editions of Torah, רְבִיעִי may look like a dark circle instead of a dark diamond.

While רְבִיעִי can stand alone, it is more often accompanied by its servant מֻנַּח. Yes, the same מֻנַּח that served אֶתְנַחְתָּא and קָטֹן. However, מֻנַּח is one of those connectors whose melody changes depending on which trope follows it. Its melody before רְבִיעִי is quite different from that before אֶתְנַחְתָּא or קָטֹן: It ascends, descends, and leads into רְבִיעִי.

Listen:

מֻנַּח ◄ רְבִיעִי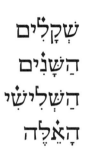

Now chant the following examples:

מֻנָּח ◂ רְבִיעִֽי

בַּיּוֹם הַשְּׁלִישִֽׁי

שְׁלֹשִׁים שְׁקָלִֽים

הַדְּבָרִים הָאֵֽלֶּה

רֹב הַשָּׁנִֽים

There is an unusual trope that may precede מֻנָּח רְבִיעִֽי. That trope resembles a normal מֻנָּח, but a vertical line (called פְּסִיק, *p'sik*) appears after the last letter of a word. This trope, called מֻנָּח לְגַרְמֵהּ (some call it simply לְגַרְמֵהּ, *l'garmeih*), looks like this:

מֻנָּח ׀

It comes before מֻנָּח רְבִיעִֽי:

Sometimes you will see what appears to be מֻנָּח ׀ לְגַרְמֵהּ before other tropes, but it is considered מֻנָּח ׀ לְגַרְמֵהּ *only before* מֻנָּח רְבִיעִֽי. In those other instances, sing the trope as מֻנָּח, *not* מֻנָּח ׀ לְגַרְמֵהּ.

The following are examples of מֻנָּח ׀ לְגַרְמֵהּ:

מֻנָּח ׀

לִפְֽי ׀

וַיְהִי ׀

כַּסְפּֽוֹ ׀

The last note of מֻנַּח | לְגַרְמֵהּ is the same as the first note of מֻנַּח רְבִיעִי. Practice the following רְבִיעִי clauses, first with tropes, then with words:

מֻנַּח | ◂ מֻנַּח ◂ רְבִיעִי

מֻנַּח ◂ רְבִיעִי

רְבִיעִי

וַיְהִי | בַּיּוֹם הַשְּׁלִישִׁי

כֶּסֶף | שְׁלֹשִׁים שְׁקָלִים

לְפִי | רֹב הַשָּׁנִים

הַדְּבָרִים הָאֵלֶּה

כִּי־יְבִיאֲךָ | יְהוָה אֱלֹהֶיךָ

יְהוָה אֱלֹהֵיכֶם

דַּרְגָּא, which you learned in lesson 7, often precedes מֻנַּח רְבִיעִי. Here are some examples of דַּרְגָּא leading to מֻנַּח רְבִיעִי. Chant the tropes first, then the words.

דַּרְגָּא ◂ מֻנַּח רְבִיעִי

שֶׁבַע פָּרֹת הַטֹּבֹת

וְהִנֵּה הַשֶּׁמֶשׁ וְהַיָּרֵחַ

To review all the tropes you have learned so far, chant the following phrases from Torah. Remember to follow the four-step approach and break down the verses into the various clauses or trope families.

הִנֵּה ׀ בֵּרַכְתִּי אֹתוֹ וְהִפְרֵיתִי אֹתוֹ וְהִרְבֵּיתִי אֹתוֹ בִּמְאֹד מְאֹד שְׁנֵים־עָשָׂר נְשִׂיאִם יוֹלִיד וּנְתַתִּיו לְגוֹי גָּדוֹל:

Behold, I have blessed him, and will make him fruitful, and will multiply him exceedingly; twelve princes shall he father, and I will make him a great nation. (Gen. 17:20)

וַיֹּאמֶר אֵלָיו אֲדֹנִי יֹדֵעַ כִּי־הַיְלָדִים רַכִּים וְהַצֹּאן וְהַבָּקָר עָלוֹת עָלָי וּדְפָקוּם יוֹם אֶחָד וָמֵתוּ כָּל־הַצֹּאן:

And he said to him, "My lord knows that the children are tender and the flocks and herds with young are with me; and if men should overdrive them one day, all the flocks will die." (Gen. 33:13)

וַיֹּאמֶר הִנֵּה חָלַמְתִּי חֲלוֹם עוֹד וְהִנֵּה הַשֶּׁמֶשׁ וְהַיָּרֵחַ וְאַחַד עָשָׂר כּוֹכָבִים מִשְׁתַּחֲוִים לִי:

He said: "Behold, I have again dreamed a dream; and, behold, the sun, and the moon, and the eleven stars made obeisance to me." (Gen. 37:9)

וַיְהִי אַחַר הַדְּבָרִים הָאֵלֶּה חָטְאוּ מַשְׁקֵה מֶלֶךְ־מִצְרַיִם וְהָאֹפֶה לַאֲדֹנֵיהֶם לְמֶלֶךְ מִצְרָיִם:

And it came to pass after these things that the butler of the king of Egypt and his baker offended their lord the king of Egypt. (Gen. 40:1)

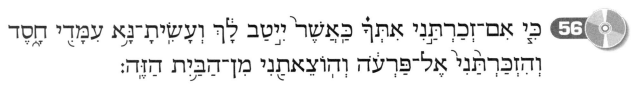

כִּי אִם־זְכַרְתַּנִי אִתְּךָ כַּאֲשֶׁר יִיטַב לָךְ וְעָשִׂיתָ־נָּא עִמָּדִי חֶסֶד וְהִזְכַּרְתַּנִי אֶל־פַּרְעֹה וְהוֹצֵאתַנִי מִן־הַבַּיִת הַזֶּה:

But think of me when it shall be well with you, and do me the kindness of mentioning me to Pharaoh, and bring me out of this place. (Gen. 40:14)

וּבַסַּל הָעֶלְיוֹן מִכֹּל מַאֲכַל פַּרְעֹה מַעֲשֵׂה אֹפֶה וְהָעוֹף אֹכֵל אֹתָם מִן־הַסַּל מֵעַל רֹאשִׁי:

And in the uppermost basket there were all kinds of baked food for Pharaoh; and the birds ate them out of the basket upon my head. (Gen. 40:17)

וַיֹּאמֶר יוֹסֵף אֶל־פַּרְעֹה חֲלוֹם פַּרְעֹה אֶחָד הוּא אֵת אֲשֶׁר הָאֱלֹהִים עֹשֶׂה הִגִּיד לְפַרְעֹה: שֶׁבַע פָּרֹת הַטֹּבֹת שֶׁבַע שָׁנִים הֵנָּה וְשֶׁבַע הַשִׁבֳּלִים הַטֹּבֹת שֶׁבַע שָׁנִים הֵנָּה חֲלוֹם אֶחָד הוּא:

And Joseph said to Pharaoh, "The dream of Pharaoh is one; God has revealed to Pharaoh what God is about to do. The seven good cows are seven years; and the seven good ears are seven years; the dream is one." (Gen. 41:25-26)

The *R'vi-i* Clause • מַעֲרֶכֶת רְבִיעִי

Part Two

Several more tropes and combinations will round out our understanding of the רְבִיעִי clause. Thus far you have encountered the connector trope קַדְמָא in two basic combinations:

1. Before מַהְפָּךְ
2. Before מֵרְכָא תְּבִיר or דַרְגָּא תְּבִיר

קַדְמָא also appears before a trope that looks like its mirror image:

When this "mirror" trope follows קַדְמָא, we call it אַזְלָא (*azla*). This combination is called קַדְמָא וְאַזְלָא (*kadma v'azla*) and sounds like this:

קַדְמָא ◄ וְאַזְלָא **57**

Practice the following examples with קַדְמָא וְאַזְלָא. For each one, chant the tropes first, then the words.

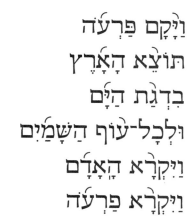

וַיָּקָם פַּרְעֹה

תּוֹצֵא הָאָרֶץ

בִדְגַת הַיָּם

וּלְכָל־עוֹף הַשָּׁמַיִם

וַיִּקְרָא הָאָדָם

וַיִּקְרָא פַּרְעֹה

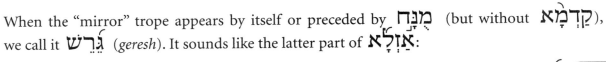

When the "mirror" trope appears by itself or preceded by מֻנָּח (but without קַדְמָא), we call it גֵּרֵשׁ (*geresh*). It sounds like the latter part of אַזְלָא:

 גֵּרֵשׁ

Both אַזְלָא and גֵּרֵשׁ are separators. גֵּרֵשׁ is often (but not always) found on words with three or fewer syllables. Chant the following examples:

הֵמָּה

אֵלֶּה

וַיַּעַשׂ

One final trope brings this section to a close: It is גֵּרְשַׁיִם (*gershayim*). It looks like a double גֵּרֵשׁ and always appears above the first letter of the last syllable of a word.

It sounds like this:

 גֵּרְשַׁיִם

Practice the following words with גֵּרְשַׁיִם:

גֵּרְשַׁיִם

וְהָיוּ

לֹא־תִכְלֶה

וְאַחֲרֵי־כֵן

וּבְקֻצְרְכֶם

גֵּרְשַׁיִם can be preceded by מֻנַּח, the same מֻנַּח you learned in lesson 7 that precedes
מֵרְכָא תְּבִיר and דַּרְגָּא תְּבִיר.

60
מֻנַּח גֵּרְשַׁיִם
אִישׁ מִזַּרְעֶךָ
פֶּה אֶל־פֶּה
יוֹם לְשָׁנָה

Practice the following combinations of tropes that can be part of the רְבִיעִי clause. If
necessary, chant the tropes separately, then chant the words.

61
וַיָּקָם פַּרְעֹה לַיְלָה
בִּדְגַת הַיָּם וּבְעוֹף הַשָּׁמַיִם
וּלְכָל־עוֹף הַשָּׁמַיִם וּלְכֹל ׀ רוֹמֵשׂ עַל־הָאָרֶץ
וַתִּקְרַבְנָה בְּנוֹת צְלָפְחָד
וַתַּעֲמֹדְנָה לִפְנֵי מֹשֶׁה
וְהָיוּ הַדְּבָרִים הָאֵלֶּה
פֶּה אֶל־פֶּה אֲדַבֶּר־בּוֹ

The following verses from Torah review most of the tropes you have learned so far. As usual,
remember to first break down each verse into clauses, chant the tropes, and then add the
melodies to the words.

62
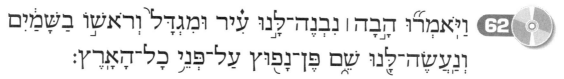
וַיֹּאמְרוּ הָבָה ׀ נִבְנֶה־לָּנוּ עִיר וּמִגְדָּל וְרֹאשׁוֹ בַשָּׁמַיִם
וְנַעֲשֶׂה־לָּנוּ שֵׁם פֶּן־נָפוּץ עַל־פְּנֵי כָל־הָאָרֶץ:

And they said, "Come, let us build us a city and a tower, whose top will reach to heaven; and
let us make a name for ourselves, lest we be scattered abroad upon the face of the whole
earth." (Gen. 11:4)

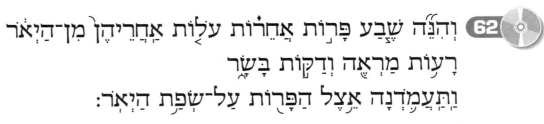

וְהִנֵּ֞ה שֶׁ֧בַע פָּר֣וֹת אֲחֵר֗וֹת עֹל֤וֹת אַחֲרֵיהֶן֙ מִן־הַיְאֹ֔ר
רָע֥וֹת מַרְאֶ֖ה וְדַקּ֣וֹת בָּשָׂ֑ר
וַֽתַּעֲמֹ֛דְנָה אֵ֥צֶל הַפָּר֖וֹת עַל־שְׂפַ֥ת הַיְאֹֽר:

And behold, seven other cows came up after them from the river, ugly and gaunt, and stood by the other cows on the brink of the river. (Gen. 41:3)

וַיִּטֹּ֣שׁ עַל־הַֽמַּחֲנֶ֡ה כְּדֶ֣רֶךְ י֣וֹם כֹּה֩ וּכְדֶ֨רֶךְ יוֹם֙ כֹּ֔ה סְבִיב֖וֹת הַֽמַּחֲנֶ֑ה
וּכְאַמָּתַ֖יִם עַל־פְּנֵ֥י הָאָֽרֶץ:

…and let them fall over the camp, about a day's journey on this side and about a day's journey on the other side, around the camp, and as it were two cubits high upon the face of the earth. (Num. 11:31)

וַתִּקְרַ֜בְנָה בְּנ֣וֹת צְלָפְחָ֗ד בֶּן־חֵ֤פֶר בֶּן־גִּלְעָד֙ בֶּן־מָכִ֣יר בֶּן־מְנַשֶּׁ֔ה
לְמִשְׁפְּחֹ֖ת מְנַשֶּׁ֣ה בֶן־יוֹסֵ֑ף
וְאֵ֙לֶּה֙ שְׁמ֣וֹת בְּנֹתָ֔יו מַחְלָ֣ה נֹעָ֔ה וְחָגְלָ֥ה וּמִלְכָּ֖ה וְתִרְצָֽה:

Then came the daughters of Zelophehad, of Manassite family—the son of Hepher, the son of Gilead, the son of Machir, the son of Manasseh, the son of Joseph. These are the names of his daughters: Mahlah, Noah, and Hoglah, and Milcah, and Tirzah. (Num. 27:1)

וָאֶקַּ֞ח אֶת־רָאשֵׁ֣י שִׁבְטֵיכֶ֗ם אֲנָשִׁ֤ים חֲכָמִים֙ וִֽידֻעִ֔ים
וָאֶתֵּ֥ן אֹתָ֛ם רָאשִׁ֖ים עֲלֵיכֶ֑ם
שָׂרֵ֨י אֲלָפִ֜ים וְשָׂרֵ֣י מֵא֗וֹת וְשָׂרֵ֤י חֲמִשִּׁים֙ וְשָׂרֵ֣י עֲשָׂרֹ֔ת
וְשֹׁטְרִ֖ים לְשִׁבְטֵיכֶֽם:

So I took the chiefs of your tribes, wise men and known, and made them chiefs over you: captains over thousands, and captains over hundreds, and captains over fifties, and captains over tens, and officers among your tribes. (Deut. 1:15)

LESSON 10

T'lisha K'tanah • תְּלִישָׁא קְטַנָּה

Pazer • פָּזֵר

T'lisha G'dolah • תְּלִישָׁא גְדוֹלָה

Before you learn the sixth and last trope clause, three tropes that appear frequently in a variety of clauses and combinations will be presented. The first, תְּלִישָׁא קְטַנָּה (*t'lisha k'tanah*), is notated above a word and looks like a circle with a small tail jutting out on its right, like this:

Like פַּשְׁטָא, תְּלִישָׁא קְטַנָּה is a "postpositive," i.e., it always appears above the last letter of a word. And just as with פַּשְׁטָא, if the word is accented somewhere other than on the final syllable, the trope will appear a second time over the accented syllable.

תְּלִישָׁא קְטַנָּה is a *m'chaber* (connector) and can be found in the *r'vi-i* clause, the *t'vir* clause, the *katon* clause, and the *segol* clause, which will be taught in the next lesson—in other words, in every clause except the *etnachta* and *sof-pasuk* clauses. The notes are close together, going down, up, up, and back down to the original note, like this:

תְּלִישָׁא קְטַנָּה

Practice the following words with תְּלִישָׁא קְטַנָּה:

תְּלִישָׁא קְטַנָּה

וַיֵּרְדוּ

וְכֹל

וַיִּבֶן

תְּלִישָׁא קְטַנָּה is often preceded (served) by מֻנַּח. This מֻנַּח jumps up and then flows right into תְּלִישָׁא קְטַנָּה. Listen:

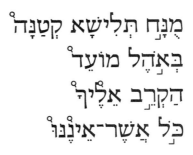

מֻנַּח תְּלִישָׁא קְטַנָּה

Chant the following combinations of מֻנַּח תְּלִישָׁא קְטַנָּה:

מֻנַּח תְּלִישָׁא קְטַנָּה

בְּאֹהֶל מוֹעֵד

הַקְרֵב אֵלֶיךָ

כָּל אֲשֶׁר־אֵינֶנּוּ

פָּזֵר (*pazer*) is the next trope you will learn in this lesson. It is a separator and may appear in almost every clause except *sof-pasuk*. It looks like an upside-down chair:

Its melody rises and then descends almost all the way back to its starting note, like this:

פָּזֵר

Chant the following words with פָּזֵר:

עֵשָׂו

אֹתָם

אֲתֹנֹת

פָּזֵר is often served by the same מֻנַּח you learned before תְּלִישָׁא קְטַנָּה.

מֻנַּח פָּזֵר   **67**

וַיִּקַּח עֵשָׂו

וְעָשָׂר אֲתֹנֹת

וְנָתַתָּה אֹתָם

תְּלִישָׁא גְדוֹלָה, the last trope in this lesson, is often confused with תְּלִישָׁא קְטַנָּה. Despite their similarity in name and appearance, the two tropes are quite different in function. Here are some ways to tell them apart:

- The little tail on תְּלִישָׁא גְדוֹלָה points to the left:

- תְּלִישָׁא גְדוֹלָה is a separator, whereas תְּלִישָׁא קְטַנָּה is a connector.

- תְּלִישָׁא גְדוֹלָה always appears over the first letter of a word; it is thus called a "prepositive." If the accent falls on a syllable other than the first, you will see a second indicating the accented syllable.

Its melody has a wider range than that of תְּלִישָׁא קְטַנָּה. It sounds a great deal like פָּזֵר but doesn't go quite as high, and it ends on the same note on which it begins:

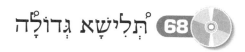

תְּלִישָׁא גְדוֹלָה   **68**

Chant the following words with תְּלִישָׁא גְדוֹלָה:

68

תְּלִישָׁא גְדוֹלָה

הָאָֽרֶץ

לֽוֹ

עֶשָׂר־יֹום

תְּלִישָׁא גְדוֹלָה is also often preceded (served) by מֻנָּח. When מֻנָּח precedes any of the three tropes presented in this chapter, it has the same melody each time:

69

מֻנָּח תְּלִישָׁא גדוֹלָה

וּלְכָל־חַיַּת הָאָֽרֶץ

בְּאַרְבָּעָה עָשָׂר־יֹום

וְנָתַתָּה אֹתָֽם

בְּאֹהֶל מוֹעֵד

Sometimes more than one מֻנָּח may precede פָּזֵר, תְּלִישָׁא קְטַנָּה, or תְּלִישָׁא גְדוֹלָה. In that case, you repeat the melody for מֻנָּח each time, as in the following examples:

70

וַיָּשֶׂם אֹתָה יוֹסֵף

אִם־יַעַבְרוּ בְנֵי־גָד וּבְנֵי־רְאוּבֵן ׀ אִתְּכֶם

אֵת כָּל־הַמִּדְבָּר הַגָּדֹל

You are now ready to chant some more complex combinations that include
תְּלִישָׁא קְטַנָּה, פָּזֵר, and תְּלִישָׁא גְדוֹלָה.

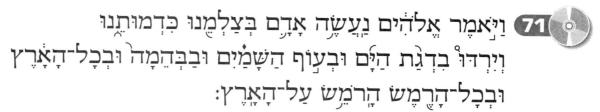

וַיֹּ֣אמֶר אֱלֹהִים֮ נַעֲשֶׂ֣ה אָדָ֛ם בְּצַלְמֵ֖נוּ כִּדְמוּתֵ֑נוּ
וְיִרְדּוּ֩ בִדְגַ֨ת הַיָּ֜ם וּבְע֣וֹף הַשָּׁמַ֗יִם וּבַבְּהֵמָה֙ וּבְכָל־הָאָ֔רֶץ
וּבְכָל־הָרֶ֖מֶשׂ הָֽרֹמֵ֥שׂ עַל־הָאָֽרֶץ:

And God said, "Let us make man in our image, after our likeness; and let them have dominion over the fish of the sea, and over the birds of the air, and over the cattle, and over all the earth, and over every creeping thing that creeps on the earth." (Gen. 1:26)

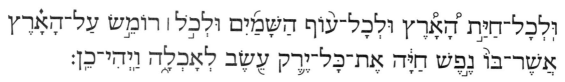

וּלְכָל־חַיַּ֣ת הָ֠אָרֶץ וּלְכָל־ע֨וֹף הַשָּׁמַ֜יִם וּלְכֹ֣ל ׀ רוֹמֵ֣שׂ עַל־הָאָ֗רֶץ
אֲשֶׁר־בּוֹ֙ נֶ֣פֶשׁ חַיָּ֔ה אֶת־כָּל־יֶ֥רֶק עֵ֖שֶׂב לְאָכְלָ֑ה וַֽיְהִי־כֵֽן:

"And to every beast of the earth, and to every bird of the air, and to everything that creeps on the earth, in which there is life, I give every green herb for food." And it was so. (Gen. 1:30)

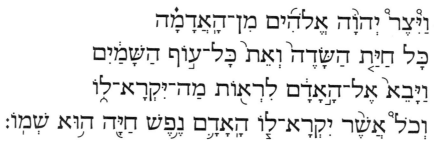

וַיִּצֶר֩ יְהֹוָ֨ה אֱלֹהִ֜ים מִן־הָֽאֲדָמָ֗ה
כָּל־חַיַּ֤ת הַשָּׂדֶה֙ וְאֵת֙ כָּל־ע֣וֹף הַשָּׁמַ֔יִם
וַיָּבֵא֙ אֶל־הָ֣אָדָ֔ם לִרְא֖וֹת מַה־יִּקְרָא־ל֑וֹ
וְכֹל֩ אֲשֶׁ֨ר יִקְרָא־ל֧וֹ הָֽאָדָ֛ם נֶ֥פֶשׁ חַיָּ֖ה ה֥וּא שְׁמֽוֹ:

And out of the earth God formed every beast of the field and every bird of the sky and brought them to Adam to see what he would call them; and whatever Adam called each living creature, that would be its name. (Gen. 2:19)

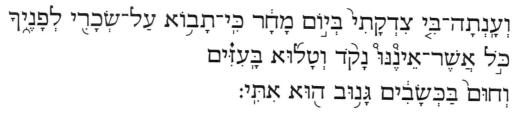

וְעָֽנְתָה־בִּ֤י צִדְקָתִי֙ בְּי֣וֹם מָחָ֔ר כִּֽי־תָב֥וֹא עַל־שְׂכָרִ֖י לְפָנֶ֑יךָ
כֹּ֣ל אֲשֶׁר־אֵינֶ֩נּוּ֩ נָקֹ֨ד וְטָל֜וּא בָּֽעִזִּ֗ים
וְחוּם֙ בַּכְּשָׂבִ֔ים גָּנ֥וּב ה֖וּא אִתִּֽי:

So shall my righteousness answer for me in time to come, when you come to look into my wages with you; every one that is not speckled and spotted among the goats, and brown among the sheep, that shall be counted stolen with me. (Gen. 30:33)

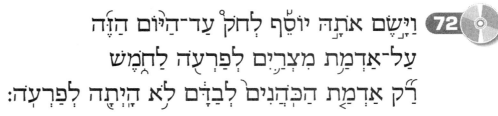

72

וַיָּ֣שֶׂם אֹתָ֣הּ יוֹסֵ֗ף לְחֹק֙ עַד־הַיּ֣וֹם הַזֶּ֔ה
עַל־אַדְמַ֥ת מִצְרַ֖יִם לְפַרְעֹ֣ה לַחֹ֑מֶשׁ
רַ֗ק אַדְמַ֤ת הַכֹּֽהֲנִים֙ לְבַדָּ֔ם לֹ֥א הָֽיְתָ֖ה לְפַרְעֹֽה׃

And Joseph made it into a land law in Egypt to this day that Pharaoh should have the fifth part; except the land of the priests only, which did not become Pharaoh's. (Gen. 47:26)

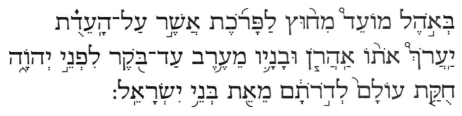

בְּאֹ֣הֶל מוֹעֵד֩ מִח֨וּץ לַפָּרֹ֜כֶת אֲשֶׁ֣ר עַל־הָעֵדֻ֗ת
יַעֲרֹךְ֩ אֹת֨וֹ אַהֲרֹ֧ן וּבָנָ֛יו מֵעֶ֥רֶב עַד־בֹּ֖קֶר לִפְנֵ֣י יְהֹוָ֑ה
חֻקַּ֤ת עוֹלָם֙ לְדֹ֣רֹתָ֔ם מֵאֵ֖ת בְּנֵ֥י יִשְׂרָאֵֽל׃

In the Tent of Meeting outside the veil, which is over the Pact, Aaron and his sons shall set it up from evening to morning before God. It shall be a statute forever to their generations on behalf of the people of Israel. (Exod. 27:21)

בְּאַרְבָּעָ֣ה עָשָׂ֧ר־י֛וֹם בַּחֹ֥דֶשׁ הַזֶּ֛ה בֵּ֥ין הָעַרְבַּ֖יִם תַּעֲשׂ֣וּ אֹת֑וֹ בְּמֹעֲד֑וֹ
כְּכׇל־חֻקֹּתָ֛יו וּכְכׇל־מִשְׁפָּטָ֖יו תַּעֲשׂ֥וּ אֹתֽוֹ׃

In the fourteenth day of this month, at evening, you shall offer it in its appointed season; according to all its rites and according to all its ceremonies shall you offer it. (Num. 9:3)

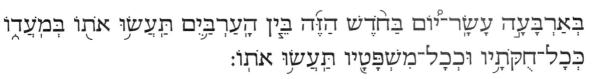
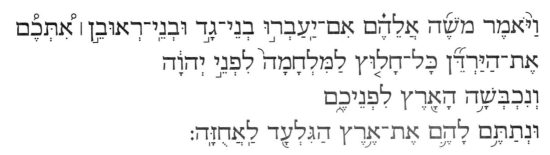

וַיֹּ֤אמֶר מֹשֶׁה֙ אֲלֵהֶ֔ם אִם־יַעַבְר֣וּ בְנֵי־גָ֣ד וּבְנֵי־רְאוּבֵ֣ן ׀ אִתְּכֶ֗ם
אֶֽת־הַיַּרְדֵּן֙ כׇּל־חָל֤וּץ לַמִּלְחָמָה֙ לִפְנֵ֣י יְהֹוָ֔ה
וְנִכְבְּשָׁ֥ה הָאָ֖רֶץ לִפְנֵיכֶ֑ם
וּנְתַתֶּ֨ם לָהֶ֜ם אֶת־אֶ֧רֶץ הַגִּלְעָ֛ד לַאֲחֻזָּֽה׃

And Moses said to them, "If the sons of Gad and the sons of Reuben will cross the Jordan with you, every man armed to battle before God, and the land shall be subdued before you, you shall give them the land of Gilead as a possession." (Num. 32:29)

The *Segol* Clause • מַעֲרֶכֶת סֶגּוֹל

So far you have learned five major families of tropes or trope clauses. You have seen that each of these clauses is governed by (and named after) the "head" trope with which the clause concludes. The clauses you have learned thus far are:

1. מַעֲרֶכֶת אֶתְנַחְתָּא   (*etnachta* clause)

2. מַעֲרֶכֶת סוֹף־פָּסוּק: (*sof-pasuk* clause)

3. מַעֲרֶכֶת קָטֹן   (*katon* clause)

4. מַעֲרֶכֶת תְּבִיר   (*t'vir* clause)

5. מַעֲרֶכֶת רְבִיעִי   (*r'vi-i* clause)

Each of the separator tropes is served by connector tropes. Although the vast majority of these connector tropes are found within many clauses, some are found only within a certain clause. For example:

מֻנָּח is found in all of them (albeit with varying melodies).

דַּרְגָּא is found in the רְבִיעִי and תְּבִיר clauses only, not in any others.

מַהְפָּך is found only in the קָטֹן clause.

In the appendix, you will find a detailed chart of all the possibilities within the clauses.

In this lesson you will learn the sixth and final trope clause, known as סֶגּוֹל (*segol*). סֶגּוֹל is the Hebrew word for "cluster," as in a cluster of grapes. The trope indeed looks like a cluster:

It sounds like this:

סֶגּוֹל

סֶגּוֹל֒ is a separator and is preceded, although not always immediately, by the connector זַרְקָא (*zarka*).

The symbol for זַרְקָא looks like this:

~

And the trope sounds like this:

זַרְקָא֮   73

Both זַרְקָא and סֶגּוֹל֒ are so-called postpositives. Just like
תְּלִישָׁא קְטַנָּה and פַּשְׁטָא, they always appear above the
last letter of a word.

If a word is accented somewhere other than on the final syllable, the trope symbol will appear a second time over the accented syllable.

You are now ready to learn the chanting of this combination, step-by-step.

First זַרְקָא֮ סֶגּוֹל֒:

זַרְקָא֮ סֶגּוֹל֒   73

וַיֹּאמֶר֮ הָאָדָם֒

וַיֵּשְׁבוּ֮ לֶאֱכָל־לֶחֶם֒

וּשְׁמַרְתֶּם֮ אֶת־הַמִּצְוֺת֒

When מֻנַּח precedes זַרְקָא֮, its melody leads right into זַרְקָא֮:

מֻנַּח ◄ זַרְקָא֮ סֶגּוֹל֒   74

וַיְסַפֵּר֮ אֶל־אָבִיו֮ וְאֶל־אֶחָיו֒

לָגוּר בָּאָרֶץ֮ בָּאנוּ֒

וְלֹא־יָכְלָה ע֖וֹד הַצְּפִינוֹ֒

מְנָח before סֶגּוֹל is a natural musical connector:

זַרְקָא ‹ מְנָח ‹ סֶגּוֹל

וְכָ֫כָה תֹּאכְלוּ אֹתוֹ

דַּבֵּר אֶל־בְּנֵי יִשְׂרָאֵל

וּמִכְנְסֵי־בַד יִלְבַּשׁ עַל־בְּשָׂרוֹ

Here are some verses from Torah that include the סֶגּוֹל clause. As the examples get longer, remember to break each verse down into its major clauses. Then practice each clause separately before you attempt to chant the entire verse.

וַיֵּשְׁבוּ֙ לֶאֱכָל־לֶ֔חֶם

וַיִּשְׂאוּ עֵינֵיהֶם וַיִּרְאוּ וְהִנֵּה֙ אֹרְחַת יִשְׁמְעֵאלִים בָּאָה מִגִּלְעָד וּגְמַלֵּיהֶם נֹשְׂאִים נְכֹאת וּצְרִי וָלֹט הוֹלְכִים לְהוֹרִיד מִצְרָיְמָה:

And they sat down to eat bread; and they lifted up their eyes and looked, and, behold, a caravan of Ishmaelites was coming from Gilead with their camels bearing gum, balm, and ladanum, going to carry them down to Egypt. (Gen. 37:25)

וַיֹּאמְרוּ אֶל־פַּרְעֹה לָגוּר בָּאָ֫רֶץ בָּ֔אנוּ

כִּי־אֵין מִרְעֶה לַצֹּאן אֲשֶׁר לַעֲבָדֶיךָ כִּי־כָבֵד הָרָעָב בְּאֶרֶץ כְּנָעַן וְעַתָּה יֵשְׁבוּ־נָא עֲבָדֶיךָ בְּאֶרֶץ גֹּשֶׁן:

They said to Pharaoh, "To sojourn in this land we have come, for your servants have no pasture for their flocks, for the famine is severe in the land of Canaan. Pray, then, let your servants stay in the land of Goshen." (Gen. 47:4)

דַּבֵּר אֶל־בְּנֵי יִשְׂרָאֵל

וְיָשֻׁבוּ֙ וְיַחֲנוּ֙ לִפְנֵי֙ פִּי הַחִירֹת בֵּין מִגְדֹּל וּבֵין הַיָּם לִפְנֵי֙ בַּעַל צְפֹן נִכְחוֹ תַחֲנוּ עַל־הַיָּם:

Speak to the people of Israel to turn back and encamp before Pihahiroth, between Migdol and the sea, opposite Baal-zephon; before it shall you encamp, by the sea. (Exod. 14:2)

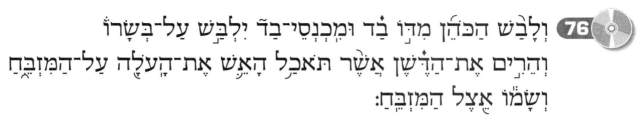

76

וְלָבַ֨שׁ הַכֹּהֵ֜ן מִדּ֣וֹ בַ֗ד וּמִכְנְסֵי־בַד֮ יִלְבַּ֣שׁ עַל־בְּשָׂרוֹ֒
וְהֵרִ֣ים אֶת־הַדֶּ֗שֶׁן אֲשֶׁ֨ר תֹּאכַ֥ל הָאֵ֛שׁ אֶת־הָעֹלָ֖ה עַל־הַמִּזְבֵּ֑חַ
וְשָׂמ֕וֹ אֵ֖צֶל הַמִּזְבֵּֽחַ׃

And the priest shall put on his linen garment, and his linen breeches shall he put upon his flesh; and he shall take up the ashes that the fire has consumed with the burnt offering on the altar, and he shall put them beside the altar. (Lev. 6:3)

There is a rare trope that sometimes appears instead of the זַרְקָ֬א סְגוֹל֒ combination. This trope is called שַׁלְשֶׁ֓לֶת (*shalshelet*) and looks like this:

The melody for שַׁלְשֶׁ֓לֶת sounds like a chain of notes, going up and down three times. Indeed, one of the meanings of the word שַׁלְשֶׁ֓לֶת is "chain."

שַׁלְשֶׁ֓לֶת **77**

שַׁלְשֶׁ֓לֶת appears only four times in the entire Torah. All four instances are listed below. First try only the words with שַׁלְשֶׁ֓לֶת; then chant the complete verses.

שַׁלְשֶׁ֓לֶת ׀

וַיִּתְמַהְמָ֓הּ ׀

וַיֹּאמַ֓ר ׀

וַיְמָאֵ֓ן ׀

וַיִּשְׁחָ֓ט ׀

Here are the complete verses.

וַיִּתְמַהְמָ֓הּ ׀ וַיַּחֲזִ֣יקוּ הָאֲנָשִׁ֣ים בְּיָד֡וֹ וּבְיַד־אִשְׁתּוֹ֩ וּבְיַ֨ד שְׁתֵּ֤י בְנֹתָיו֙
בְּחֶמְלַ֥ת יְהוָ֖ה עָלָ֑יו וַיֹּצִאֻ֥הוּ וַיַּנִּחֻ֖הוּ מִח֥וּץ לָעִֽיר׃

Still he lingered; so the men seized his hand and the hand of his wife and of his two
daughters, God being merciful to him; and they brought him and left him outside the city.
(Gen. 19:16)

וַיֹּאמַ֓ר ׀ יְהוָ֗ה אֱלֹהֵי֙ אֲדֹנִ֣י אַבְרָהָ֔ם הַקְרֵה־נָ֥א לְפָנַ֖י הַיּ֑וֹם
וַעֲשֵׂה־חֶ֕סֶד עִ֖ם אֲדֹנִ֥י אַבְרָהָֽם׃

And he said, "O *Adonai*, God of my master Abraham, I beseech you, send me good speed
this day and show kindness to my master Abraham." (Gen. 24:12)

וַיְמָאֵ֓ן ׀ וַיֹּ֙אמֶר֙ אֶל־אֵ֣שֶׁת אֲדֹנָ֔יו הֵ֣ן אֲדֹנִ֔י לֹא־יָדַ֥ע אִתִּ֖י מַה־בַּבָּ֑יִת
וְכֹ֥ל אֲשֶׁר־יֶשׁ־ל֖וֹ נָתַ֥ן בְּיָדִֽי׃

But he refused; and he said to his master's wife, "Look, with me here, my master gives no
thought to anything in this house, and all that he owns he has placed in my hands."
(Gen. 39:8)

וַיִּשְׁחָ֓ט ׀ וַיִּקַּ֣ח מֹשֶׁ֣ה מִדָּמ֗וֹ וַיִּתֵּ֛ן עַל־תְּנ֥וּךְ אֹֽזֶן־אַהֲרֹ֖ן הַיְמָנִ֑ית
וְעַל־בֹּ֤הֶן יָדוֹ֙ הַיְמָנִ֔ית וְעַל־בֹּ֥הֶן רַגְל֖וֹ הַיְמָנִֽית׃

And he slew it; and Moses took of its blood and put it on the tip of Aaron's right ear, and on
the thumb of his right hand, and on the big toe of his right foot. (Lev. 8:23)

Karnei Parah • קַרְנֵי פָּרָה

Yare-ach Ben Yomo • יָרֵחַ בֶּן יוֹמוֹ

These last two tropes appear together and occur only one time in the entire Torah—during the reading of the final פָּרָשָׁה (weekly portion) of the Book of Numbers, the portion known as מַסְעֵי. Toward the end of the פָּרָשָׁה, in Numbers 35:5, there is a discussion about land that will be set aside for the tribe of Levi. In the course of the discussion, God prescribes specific measurements of pasture land for the tribe. It is in this context that these two uncommon tropes appear.

The first trope is the separator קַרְנֵי פָּרָה (*karnei parah*), which looks exactly—and sounds exactly—like a תְּלִישָׁא קְטַנָּה and a תְּלִישָׁא גְדוֹלָה stuck together:

Try to chant these two tropes, one after the other:

תְּלִישָׁא קְטַנָּה   תְּלִישָׁא גְדוֹלָה

That is exactly how this new rare trope sounds—first the melody of תְּלִישָׁא־קְטַנָּה   and then the melody of תְּלִישָׁא גְדוֹלָה:

 קַרְנֵי פָּרָה

And here is the only example from Torah:

 בָּאַמָּה

The second trope is יָרֵחַ בֶּן יוֹמוֹ (*yare-ach ben yomo*), which looks like an upside-down *etnachta* but sounds like a *munach* before תְּלִישָׁא גְדוֹלָה:

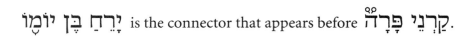

יָרֵחַ בֶּן יוֹמוֹ is the connector that appears before 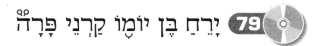 קַרְנֵי פָרָה.

Together they sound like this:

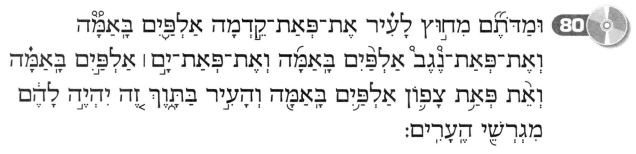

79 יָרֵחַ בֶּן יוֹמוֹ קַרְנֵי פָרָה

And here is the entire verse:

80 וּמַדֹּתֶם מִחוּץ לָעִיר אֶת־פְּאַת־קֵדְמָה אַלְפַּיִם בָּאַמָּה
וְאֶת־פְּאַת־נֶגֶב אַלְפַּיִם בָּאַמָּה וְאֶת־פְּאַת־יָם ׀ אַלְפַּיִם בָּאַמָּה
וְאֵת פְּאַת צָפוֹן אַלְפַּיִם בָּאַמָּה וְהָעִיר בַּתָּוֶךְ זֶה יִהְיֶה לָהֶם
מִגְרְשֵׁי הֶעָרִים:

And you shall measure off outside the city on the east side two thousand cubits, and on the
south side two thousand cubits, and on the west side two thousand cubits, and on the north
side two thousand cubits, and the city shall be in the midst. This shall be the pasture for
their cities. (Num. 35:5)

YOU CAN CHANT TORAH!

As you begin to prepare Torah portions, you will no doubt find that there is a vast amount of material to cover. In this chapter we offer some guidelines that have been found useful for tackling a Torah reading in the most effective way.

We'll look first at Numbers 35:3 because this verse presents some typical and interesting trope combinations for us to study.

וְהָי֣וּ הֶעָרִ֤ים לָהֶם֙ לָשֶׁ֔בֶת וּמִגְרְשֵׁיהֶ֕ם יִהְי֕וּ לִבְהֶמְתָּם֙

וְלִרְכֻשָׁ֕ם וּלְכֹ֖ל חַיָּתָֽם:

And they shall have the cities to live in; and their pasture shall be for their cattle, and for their goods, and for all their beasts. (Num. 35:3)

1. Be sure that you read the Hebrew text correctly. Did you see the penultimate accent on the word לָשֶׁ֔בֶת? Were you sure to say וּמִגְרְשֵׁיהֶ֕ם, *oomigr'sheihem*, and not *oomigr'sheichem*?

2. It's a good idea to look through the verse, separating the trope clauses so that you have an idea of its overall structure. In this particular verse you should have counted five clauses:

   • A *t'vir* clause ending with the word הֶעָרִ֤ים

   • An *etnachta* clause ending with the word לָשֶׁ֔בֶת

   • A *r'vi-i* clause on the single word וּמִגְרְשֵׁיהֶ֕ם

   • A *katon* clause ending with the word וְלִרְכֻשָׁ֕ם

   • The *sof-pasuk* clause ending the verse with the word חַיָּתָֽם:

3. Chant the tropes carefully, if necessary clause by clause.

4. Chant the words.

Since you're thirsting for more examples, let's turn to Exodus 17:3 and meet some more people who are thirsting.

וַיִּצְמָ֨א שָׁ֤ם הָעָם֙ לַמַּ֔יִם וַיָּ֤לֶן הָעָם֙ עַל־מֹשֶׁ֔ה וַיֹּ֕אמֶר לָ֤מָּה זֶּה֙
הֶעֱלִיתָ֣נוּ מִמִּצְרַ֔יִם לְהָמִ֥ית אֹתִ֛י וְאֶת־בָּנַ֥י וְאֶת־מִקְנַ֖י בַּצָּמָֽא׃

But the people thirsted there for water; and the people murmured against Moses and said, "Why have you brought us up out of Egypt, to kill us and our children and our cattle with thirst?" (Exod. 17:3)

1. Read the words. The first word is וַיִּצְמָ֨א—vayitzma, not vayimtza. וַיָּ֤לֶן is stressed on the second syllable. So are וַיֹּ֕אמֶר and לַמַּ֔יִם.

2. Analyze the clauses:
   - The *katon* clause ends on the fourth word of the verse, לַמַּ֔יִם.
   - The *etnachta* clause ends three words later with עַל־מֹשֶׁ֔ה.
   - The single word וַיֹּ֕אמֶר is the *r'vi-i* clause.
   - The *katon* clause ends four words later with מִמִּצְרַ֔יִם.
   - Then there is a two-word *t'vir* clause ending with אֹתִ֛י.
   - The verse concludes with בַּצָּמָֽא׃.

3. Chant the tropes. Make sure you chant the first trope as קַדְמָ֨א. You can clearly see that it's *not* over the last letter and that it is followed by *mapach*. The rest of the tropes are straightforward.

4. Chant the words.

There's just one more step, and that is to prepare yourself for reading from the unvocalized calligraphy in the Torah scroll. The prospect of chanting without vowels and trope signs may seem daunting. But as you may have noticed at the end of lessons 2 and 5, once you've prepared the Hebrew well, it's not that difficult. In fact, you probably have memorized many of the vowels and tropes without even realizing it!

People have different learning styles. In general, we've found that most people do well by taking a small amount of material—a verse or two or three verses—preparing that material thoroughly according to the four-step process, then trying it in the Torah calligraphy, or what we'll call the Torah script. For example, here is the last passage we've analyzed. You'll probably find that you've memorized a lot of it, but not all. So you'll want to go back to the Hebrew and practice until you are 100 percent comfortable chanting it from the vocalized version. We recommend that you study small amounts of material during short but very frequent periods of time.

ויצמא שם העם למים וילן העם על משה ויאמר למה זה
העליתנו ממצרים להמית אתי ואת בני ואת מקני בצמא

From the *Encyclopedia of Judaism*, Eliyahu Schleifer, Jerusalem, 1989

Cantillation   The art of the liturgical chanting of the Bible. Jewish liturgical regulations require that various portions of the Bible be read ceremoniously in public services. Portions of the Pentateuch are read during the morning services on Mondays, Thursdays, Saturdays, New Moons, Festivals, and the High Holidays. A portion from the Prophets is read on Saturdays, Festivals, and Holidays (this portion is called the *haftarah*). Other books are read on appropriate occasions: the Scrolls of Song of Songs, Ruth, and Ecclesiastes on the Three Pilgrim Festivals; the Scroll of Esther on Purim; and Lamentations on the Ninth of Av (*Tishah B'av*).

The public reading of the Pentateuch and the Scrolls is usually executed by a professional or semiprofessional reader called a *ba-al k'ree-ah or ba-al koreh* (in the Yemenite tradition the Pentateuch is read by laymen), and with the exception of some Reform synagogues, the reading is always chanted. The art of chanting is ancient and may date back to Second Temple times, but the different melodic patterns used by the various Jewish communities developed much later, perhaps during the Middle Ages, and have continued to grow and change ever since.

The cantillation of Scripture is expected to adhere to the signs called *t'amim or ta-amei hamikra*. These were developed together with the punctuation signs in Babylonia and Eretz Yisrael during the talmudic and post-talmudic periods; they were first transmitted orally and were later codified in various notation systems, the fullest and most important of which was the one developed by the Masoretic school of Tiberias in the ninth and tenth centuries C.E. The Tiberian sages assigned three functions to the accents (*t'amim*): (a) to show the proper accentuation of the words; (b) to divide the biblical verses properly and thus help preserve the acceptable interpretation of the text; and (c) to indicate the melodic patterns that should be used with each part of the verse. Because of this last function, the signs are also called *n'ginot* (melodies). The codices compiled by these scholars (the most famous of which are the *Crown of Aleppo*, c.920 C.E., now in Jerusalem, and the *Leningrad Codex*, c.1010) have been accepted as the authorized versions of the Hebrew Bible.

The signs of the accents are marked only in the Masoretic codices and in the printed Bibles. They are never copied in the scrolls that are used for the liturgical reading in the synagogue. In most communities it is customary to read the portion of the Prophets from a codex or a printed Bible, but the Pentateuch and the Five Scrolls are read from scrolls. In the latter cases, the reader is obliged to memorize the signs in order to effect a correct cantillation. As a practicing device, modern readers use a book called *tikkun lakorim*, which contains the original text as written in the scroll side by side with the Masoretic version, which includes the punctuation and accents, in two parallel columns. An earlier means of overcoming the lack of accents in the scrolls was the use of a prompter (*somech*), who indicated the accents to the reader by a system of hand signals called cheironomy. Some of the accents may have derived their names from the cheironomical signals that accompany them. Cheironomy is still in use in some Jewish communities, with some preserving the old customs and others inventing new methods.

The Masoretic accents of Tiberias are organized into two graphical systems: one for the Psalms, Proverbs, and the central part of Job and a second system for the other twenty-one books of the Bible. Only the latter is relevant to the ceremonial reading of Scripture in public. The system contains twenty-eight signs, most of which are written above and some below the letters, and one sign follows the relevant word. The signs are classified as (a) Disjunctives or Lords, which mark the end of verses and divide the latter into phrases, clauses, and subclauses; and (b) Conjunctives, or Servants, whose task is to link the words within the division or subdivision of a verse. The Disjunctives are hierarchical, based on the degree of closure that they affect. Their placement in the text was determined by syntactical, exegetical, and musical considerations.

The signs of the *t'amim* are universally accepted by all Jews. However, their musical interpretation differs from one community to the next. One can speak of eight main musical traditions of cantillation:

1. Southern Arab Peninsula: Yemen and Hadramaut. This is perhaps one of the oldest traditions of cantillation. Theoretically it recognizes all the signs of the *t'amim*, but in practice, some are not used. The style of chanting may suggest that the tradition is based on an earlier system of cantillation, such as was recorded in the Babylonian notation during the seventh century and earlier.

2. The Middle East: Iran, Bukhara, Kurdistan, Georgia, and the northern parts of Iraq. Another old tradition, perhaps based partially on the old Babylonian system of notation but musically different from the Yemenite tradition.

3. The Near East: Turkey, Syria, central Iraq, Lebanon, and Egypt. This is known as the Eastern Sephardic Tradition. It can be heard in some Greek and Balkan communities

and has become the dominant style of the non-Ashkenazi communities of Israel. The readers of the Pentateuch strive to give musical meaning to each sign, but some of the signs are ignored in the reading of the Prophets and other books. The musical motives are influenced by the Arabic modes of the *maqam*.

4. North Africa: Libya, Tunisia, Algeria, and Morocco. This tradition reflects the influence of African pentatonic patterns, especially in communities far from the shores of the Mediterranean.

5. Italy. The ancient tradition of the Italian Jews can still be heard in Rome and in the Roman Jewish community of Jerusalem. Cheironomy is still used by some of those readers.

6. The Sephardic and Portuguese communities of Europe. The so-called Western Sephardim may preserve the main features of the original Sephardic cantillation melodies.

7. Western European Ashkenazim: German-speaking countries, France, some communities of the Netherlands, and England. This tradition, which developed in medieval times, was first recorded in European cantorial manuals of the nineteenth century.

8. East-European Ashkenazim. This tradition developed out of the Western Ashkenazi cantillation and has become the dominant style among the Ashkenazi communities of Israel and English-speaking countries. The Lithuanian version of this tradition is perhaps the most meticulous musical system in existence.

Most of the eight musical traditions have diverse subtraditions. Considerable musical differences exist among the various countries within one tradition and even different parts of the same country. In addition, each tradition has different melodic patterns for various divisions of the Bible or for different liturgical occasions. Thus, for example, the East-European Ashkenazi tradition consists of six musical systems: the regular Pentateuch reading; the High Holiday version of the same; the Prophets; the Book of Esther; the Song of Songs, Ruth, and Ecclesiastes; and Lamentations.

We have spoken of the tropes either as מַפְסִיקִים, separators, or מְחַבְּרִים, connectors. The separators may bring a phrase to a temporary pause — like טִפְחָא—or to an undeniably final cadence—like סוֹף־פָּסוּק. The connectors—like מֵרְכָא and מַהְפָּךְ—bind words together and insure an uninterrupted flow within a phrase.

An analysis of the first verse of the Torah illustrates the contrasting functions of מְחַבְּרִים and מַפְסִיקִים. The function of each trope is notated beneath the symbol.

הָאָרֶץ׃	וְאֵת	הַשָּׁמַיִם	אֵת	אֱלֹהִים	בָּרָא	בְּרֵאשִׁית
(‖ *mafsik* ◄	*m'chaber* |	*mafsik* ◄	*m'chaber* |	*mafsik* ◄	*m'chaber* |	*mafsik*)
separator	connector	separator	connector	separator	connector	separator

The English translation demonstrates the elegant manner in which the tropes fulfill their most important function—revealing the meaning of the sacred text:

> In the beginning   God created   the heavens   and the earth.

You may have noticed that the space or pause after "In the beginning" is half as long as the space or pause after "created." This is due to the fact that while אֶתְנַחְתָּא and טִפְחָא are both מַפְסִיקִים, אֶתְנַחְתָּא is the stronger one. It is considered an "emperor," while טִפְחָא is considered a "king," one rung lower in the cantillation "hierarchy." When you chant this verse, you will want to pause considerably after *sof-pasuk*, clearly pause after *etnachta*, and pause slightly after *tipcha*. If you do this, the meaning of the words will become clear.

On the following pages you will find two different tables. The first one lists all of the טַעֲמֵי הַמִּקְרָא, their symbols, names, and meanings—first the מַפְסִיקִים in hierarchical order and then the מְחַבְּרִים.

   The second table shows all of the trope clauses or families, listing all the tropes you may find in each clause and the relationships among them.

TROPE TABLE A

"Hierarchy"	Symbol	Name	Meaning
"Emperors" (long pause)		סוֹף־פָּסוּק sof-pasuk	end of sentence
		אֶתְנַחְתָּא etnachta	to rest
"Kings" (shorter pause than "Emperors")		סֶגוֹל segol	cluster
		שַׁלְשֶׁלֶת shalshelet	chain
		(זָקֵף) קָטֹן (zakef) katon	lesser upright
		זָקֵף גָדוֹל zakef gadol	full upright
		רְבִיעִי r'vi-i	four-square
"Dukes" Shorter pause than "Kings")		טִפְּחָא tipcha	handbreath
		פַּשְׁטָא pashta	extending
		יְתִיב y'tiv	staying
		זַרְקָא zarka	scattered
		מֻנַח l לְגַרְמֵהּ munach l'garmeih	independent *munach*
"Officers" (shorter pause than "Dukes")		תְּבְר t'vir	broken
		גֶרֶשׁ geresh	to chase
		אַזְלָא azla	going on
		גֵרְשַׁיִם gershayim	double *geresh*
		פָּזֵר pazer	to scatter
		תְּלִישָׁא גְדוֹלָה t'lisha g'dolah	big *t'lisha*
		קַרְנֵי פָּרָה karnei parah	horns of a heifer
		מֵרְכָא mercha	to lengthen
		מֻנַח munach	sustained
		מַהְפַּךְ mapach	reversed
		קַדְמָא kadma	to proceed
		דַּרְגָּא darga	stepwise
		תְּלִישָׁא קְטַנָה t'lisha k'tanah	small *t'lisha*
		יָרֵחַ בֶּן יוֹמוֹ yare-ach ben yomo	moon of one day
		מֵרְכָא כְּפוּלָה mercha k'fulah	double *mercha*

(Left margin labels: MAFSIKIM (Separators), M'CHABRIM (Conectors))

TROPE TABLE B

I *Sof-Pasuk* Clause

Name	Symbol	Function	Serves	Served by
sof-pasuk		mafsik		tipcha mercha
tipcha		mafsik	sof-pasuk	mercha
mercha		m'chaber	sof-pasuk tipcha	

II *Etnachta* Clause

Name	Symbol	Function	Serves	Served by
etnachta		mafsik		tipcha munach
tipcha		mafsik	etnachta	mercha
munach		m'chaber	etnachta	
mercha		m'chaber	tipcha	

III *Katon* Clause

Name	Symbol	Function	Serves	Served by
katon		mafsik		munach pashta y'tiv
pashta		mafsik	katon	mapach mercha
munach		m'chaber	katon mapach	
mapach		m'chaber	pashta	munach
kadma		m'chaber	mapach	
zakef gadol		mafsik		
y'tiv		mafsik	munach katon	
t'lisha g'dolah		mafsik		munach

IV *T'vir* Clause

Name	Symbol	Function	Serves	Served by
t'vir	֯	mafsik		darga mercha
darga	֯	m'chaber	t'vir	munach kadma
mercha	֯	m'chaber	t'vir	munach kadma
mercha k'fulah	֯	m'chaber		darga
munach	֯	m'chaber	darga mercha t'lisha k'tanah	
kadma	֯	m'chaber	darga mercha	
t'lisha k'tanah	֯	m'chaber	kadma	munach
gershayim	֯	mafsik		munach

V *R'vi-i* Clause

Name	Symbol	Function	Serves	Served by
r'vi-i	֯	mafsik		munach kadma v'azla gershayim
munach l'garmeih	֯	mafsik	munach r'vi-i	darga kadma v'azla geresh
azla	֯	mafsik		kadma
munach	֯	m'chaber	r'vi-i	munach l'garmeih darga kadma v'azla geresh gershayim
kadma	֯	m'chaber	azla	t'lisha k'tanah
gershayim	֯	mafsik		munach

V *R'vi-i* Clause (continued)

Name	Symbol	Function	Serves	Served by
geresh	⌐	mafsik		munach kadma t'lisha g'dolah
darga	⟋	m'chaber	munach r'vi-i	munach kadma
pazer	ד	mafsik		munach
t'lisha k'tanah	۹	m'chaber	kadma	munach
yare-ach ben yomo	⌣	m'chaber	karnei-farah	munach
karnei parah	۹۹	mafsik		yare-ach ben yomo

VI *Segol* Clause

Name	Symbol	Function	Serves	Served by
segol	∴	mafsik		zarka munach
zarka	~	m'chaber	segol	munach
munach	⌐	m'chaber	segol zarka	
shalshelet	⅏	mafsik		
mercha	⌐	m'chaber	zarka	
kadma	⌐	m'chaber	munach mercha	

In some sections of the Torah, special melodies are used instead of the regular cantillation, or the tropes are interpreted in a slightly different way. The most frequently occurring example is the one you learned at the end of lesson 2, the *sof-aliyah*, in which the last *sof-pasuk* clause of each *aliyah* is chanted to a special melody. In this appendix, some other such instances in the Torah are discussed.

שִׁירַת הַיָּם

The "Song of the Sea" is found in the portion of the Book of Exodus called *B'shalach*. There are many different traditions related to the reading of these verses, Exodus 15:1-19. In some communities, like the Spanish-Portuguese, the cantillation is virtually disregarded, and a completely new melody accompanies the words. In most Ashkenazi communities, however, a special melody is used for each phrase in the song that has God's name in it. This melody is somewhat tied to the tropes but doesn't follow the cantillation exactly.

In the following text you will see in bold those phrases that are sung to the special melody. The rest of the text follows the regular trope that you have learned. On the recording you will hear the first three verses chanted. Notice the contrast between the *Shirat Hayam* melody and the regular trope.

81

אָ֣ז יָשִֽׁיר־מֹשֶׁה֩ וּבְנֵ֨י יִשְׂרָאֵ֜ל אֶת־הַשִּׁירָ֤ה הַזֹּאת֙ לַֽיהוָ֔ה וַיֹּאמְר֖וּ

סוּס **אָשִׁ֤ירָה לַֽיהוָה֙ כִּֽי־גָאֹ֣ה גָּאָ֔ה** לֵאמֹ֑ר

וְרֹכְב֖וֹ רָמָ֥ה בַיָּֽם: עָזִּ֤י וְזִמְרָת֙ יָ֔הּ וַֽיְהִי־לִ֖י

אֱלֹהֵ֥י **זֶ֤ה אֵלִי֙ וְאַנְוֵ֔הוּ** לִֽישׁוּעָ֑ה

אָבִ֖י וַאֲרֹמְמֶֽנְהוּ: **יְהוָ֖ה אִ֣ישׁ מִלְחָמָ֑ה יְהוָ֖ה**

וּמִבְחַ֥ר **שְׁמֽוֹ: מַרְכְּבֹ֥ת פַּרְעֹ֛ה וְחֵיל֖וֹ יָרָ֣ה בַיָּ֑ם**

כְּמוֹ־ **שָׁלִשָׁ֖יו טֻבְּע֥וּ בְיַם־סֽוּף: תְּהֹמֹ֖ת יְכַסְיֻ֑מוּ יָרְד֥וּ בִמְצוֹלֹ֖ת**

יְמִֽינְךָ֥ **אָֽבֶן: יְמִֽינְךָ֣ יְהוָ֔ה נֶאְדָּרִ֖י בַּכֹּ֑חַ**

יְהוָ֖ה תִּרְעַ֥ץ אוֹיֵֽב: **וּבְרֹ֥ב גְּאֽוֹנְךָ֖ תַּהֲרֹ֣ס**

קָמֶ֑יךָ תְּשַׁלַּח֙ חֲרֹ֣נְךָ֔ יֹאכְלֵ֖מוֹ כַּקַּֽשׁ: וּבְר֤וּחַ

אַפֶּ֨יךָ֙ נֶ֣עֶרְמוּ מַ֔יִם נִצְּב֥וּ כְמוֹ־נֵ֖ד

נֹזְלִ֑ים קָֽפְא֥וּ תְהֹמֹ֖ת בְּלֶב־יָֽם: אָמַ֣ר

אוֹיֵ֛ב אֶרְדֹּ֥ף אַשִּׂ֖יג אֲחַלֵּ֣ק שָׁלָ֑ל תִּמְלָאֵ֣מוֹ

נַפְשִׁ֔י אָרִ֣יק חַרְבִּ֔י תּוֹרִישֵׁ֖מוֹ יָדִֽי: נָשַׁ֣פְתָּ

בְרוּחֲךָ֖ כִּסָּ֣מוֹ יָ֑ם צָלֲלוּ֙ כַּֽעוֹפֶ֔רֶת בְּמַ֖יִם

אַדִּירִֽים: **מִֽי־כָמֹ֤כָה בָּֽאֵלִם֙ יְהֹוָ֔ה** **מִ֥י**

כָּמֹ֖כָה נֶאְדָּ֣ר בַּקֹּ֑דֶשׁ **נוֹרָ֥א תְהִלֹּ֖ת עֹ֥שֵׂה**

פֶֽלֶא: נָטִ֙יתָ֙ יְמִ֣ינְךָ֔ תִּבְלָעֵ֖מוֹ אָֽרֶץ: נָחִ֥יתָ

בְחַסְדְּךָ֖ עַם־ז֣וּ גָּאָ֑לְתָּ נֵהַ֥לְתָּ בְעָזְּךָ֖ אֶל־נְוֵ֥ה

קָדְשֶֽׁךָ: שָֽׁמְע֥וּ עַמִּ֖ים יִרְגָּז֑וּן חִ֣יל

אָחַ֕ז יֹשְׁבֵ֖י פְּלָֽשֶׁת: אָ֚ז נִבְהֲלוּ֙ אַלּוּפֵ֣י

אֱד֔וֹם אֵילֵ֣י מוֹאָ֔ב יֹֽאחֲזֵ֖מוֹ רָ֑עַד נָמֹ֕גוּ

כֹּ֖ל יֹשְׁבֵ֥י כְנָֽעַן: תִּפֹּ֨ל עֲלֵיהֶ֜ם אֵימָ֣תָה

וָפַ֗חַד בִּגְדֹ֤ל זְרֽוֹעֲךָ֙ יִדְּמ֣וּ כָּאָ֑בֶן **עַד־**

יַעֲבֹ֤ר עַמְּךָ֙ יְהֹוָ֔ה **עַד־יַעֲבֹ֖ר עַם־ז֥וּ**

קָנִֽיתָ: תְּבִאֵ֗מוֹ וְתִטָּעֵ֙מוֹ֙ בְּהַ֣ר נַחֲלָֽתְךָ֔ מָכ֧וֹן

לְשִׁבְתְּךָ֛ פָּעַ֖לְתָּ יְהֹוָ֑ה מִקְּדָ֕שׁ אֲדֹנָ֖י כּוֹנְנ֥וּ

יָדֶֽיךָ: **יְהֹוָ֥ה ׀ יִמְלֹ֖ךְ לְעֹלָ֥ם וָעֶֽד:** כִּ֣י

בָא֩ ס֨וּס פַּרְעֹ֜ה בְּרִכְבּ֤וֹ וּבְפָרָשָׁיו֙ בַּיָּ֔ם וַיָּ֧שֶׁב יְהֹוָ֛ה עֲלֵהֶ֖ם

אֶת־מֵ֣י הַיָּ֑ם וּבְנֵ֧י יִשְׂרָאֵ֛ל הָלְכ֥וּ בַיַּבָּשָׁ֖ה בְּת֥וֹךְ הַיָּֽם:

וַתִּקַּח֩ מִרְיָ֨ם הַנְּבִיאָ֜ה אֲח֧וֹת אַהֲרֹ֛ן אֶת־הַתֹּ֖ף בְּיָדָ֑הּ וַתֵּצֶ֤אןָ

כָל־הַנָּשִׁים֙ אַחֲרֶ֔יהָ בְּתֻפִּ֖ים וּבִמְחֹלֹֽת: וַתַּ֥עַן לָהֶ֖ם מִרְיָ֑ם

שִׁ֤ירוּ לַֽיהֹוָה֙ כִּֽי־גָאֹ֣ה גָּאָ֔ה ס֥וּס וְרֹכְב֖וֹ רָמָ֥ה בַיָּֽם:

The Ten Commandments עֲשֶׂרֶת הַדִּבְּרוֹת

The Ten Commandments occur twice in the Torah—once in the section from Exodus called *Yitro* (Exod. 20:1-14) and once in the section from Deuteronomy called *Va-etchanan* (Deut. 5:6-18). You may notice that most words in both these portions have two sets of tropes! This may seem confusing at first, but actually there is a simple explanation. One set is called *ta-amei ha-elyon* (the upper trope) and the other *ta-amei hatachton* (the lower trope). *Ta-amei ha-elyon* are used for public reading in the synagogue. They make each commandment into one (long or short) verse. *Ta-amei hatachton* are used only for private study; in this instance, the tropes divide most of the commandments into verses of average length.

For the *ta-amei ha-elyon*, you chant the tropes that are mostly above the words.

Many sources, in fact, print the text with each set of tropes presented separately. For your reference, here are both versions of the Ten Commandments with both versions of the tropes.

בְּטַעַם הָעֶלְיוֹן • Ex. 20:2–14	בְּטַעַם הַתַּחְתּוֹן • Ex. 20:2–14

אָנֹכִי יְהֹוָה אֱלֹהֶיךָ אֲשֶׁר הוֹצֵאתִיךָ
מֵאֶרֶץ מִצְרַיִם מִבֵּית עֲבָדִים לֹא־
יִהְיֶה לְךָ אֱלֹהִים אֲחֵרִים עַל־
פָּנָי לֹא־תַעֲשֶׂה לְךָ פֶסֶל וְכָל־
תְּמוּנָה אֲשֶׁר בַּשָּׁמַיִם מִמַּעַל
וַאֲשֶׁר בָּאָרֶץ מִתַּחַת וַאֲשֶׁר בַּמַּיִם
מִתַּחַת לָאָרֶץ לֹא־תִשְׁתַּחֲוֶה
לָהֶם וְלֹא תָעָבְדֵם כִּי אָנֹכִי יְהֹוָה
אֱלֹהֶיךָ אֵל קַנָּא פֹּקֵד עֲוֺן אָבֹת עַל־בָּנִים עַל־שִׁלֵּשִׁים וְעַל־רִבֵּעִים
לְשֹׂנְאָי וְעֹשֶׂה חֶסֶד לַאֲלָפִים
לְאֹהֲבַי וּלְשֹׁמְרֵי מִצְוֹתָי לֹא תִשָּׂא אֶת־שֵׁם־יְהֹוָה אֱלֹהֶיךָ
לַשָּׁוְא כִּי לֹא יְנַקֶּה יְהֹוָה אֵת אֲשֶׁר־יִשָּׂא אֶת־שְׁמוֹ לַשָּׁוְא
זָכוֹר אֶת־יוֹם הַשַּׁבָּת לְקַדְּשׁוֹ
שֵׁשֶׁת יָמִים תַּעֲבֹד וְעָשִׂיתָ כָּל־
מְלַאכְתֶּךָ וְיוֹם הַשְּׁבִיעִי שַׁבָּת
לַיהֹוָה אֱלֹהֶיךָ לֹא תַעֲשֶׂה כָל־
מְלָאכָה אַתָּה וּבִנְךָ וּבִתֶּךָ עַבְדְּךָ
וַאֲמָתְךָ וּבְהֶמְתֶּךָ וְגֵרְךָ אֲשֶׁר
בִּשְׁעָרֶיךָ כִּי שֵׁשֶׁת־יָמִים עָשָׂה
יְהֹוָה אֶת־הַשָּׁמַיִם וְאֶת־הָאָרֶץ אֶת־הַיָּם וְאֶת־כָּל־אֲשֶׁר־בָּם
וַיָּנַח בַּיּוֹם הַשְּׁבִיעִי עַל־כֵּן בֵּרַךְ יְהֹוָה אֶת־יוֹם הַשַּׁבָּת וַיְקַדְּשֵׁהוּ
כַּבֵּד אֶת־אָבִיךָ וְאֶת־אִמֶּךָ לְמַעַן יַאֲרִכוּן יָמֶיךָ
עַל הָאֲדָמָה אֲשֶׁר־יְהֹוָה אֱלֹהֶיךָ נֹתֵן לָךְ
לֹא תִרְצָח לֹא תִנְאָף לֹא תִגְנֹב
לֹא־תַעֲנֶה בְרֵעֲךָ עֵד שָׁקֶר
לֹא תַחְמֹד בֵּית רֵעֶךָ לֹא־תַחְמֹד אֵשֶׁת רֵעֶךָ
וְעַבְדּוֹ וַאֲמָתוֹ וְשׁוֹרוֹ וַחֲמֹרוֹ וְכֹל אֲשֶׁר לְרֵעֶךָ

בְּטַעַם הָעֶלְיוֹן • Deut. 5:6–18

אָנֹכִי יְהוָֹה אֱלֹהֶיךָ אֲשֶׁר הוֹצֵאתִיךָ
מֵאֶרֶץ מִצְרַיִם מִבֵּית עֲבָדִים: לֹא
יִהְיֶה־לְךָ אֱלֹהִים אֲחֵרִים עַל־
פָּנָי לֹא תַעֲשֶׂה־לְךָ פֶסֶל ׀ כָּל־
תְּמוּנָה אֲשֶׁר בַּשָּׁמַיִם ׀ מִמַּעַל
וַאֲשֶׁר בָּאָרֶץ מִתַּחַת וַאֲשֶׁר בַּמַּיִם ׀
מִתַּחַת לָאָרֶץ לֹא־תִשְׁתַּחֲוֶה
לָהֶם וְלֹא תָעָבְדֵם כִּי אָנֹכִי יְהוָֹה
אֱלֹהֶיךָ אֵל קַנָּא פֹּקֵד עֲוֹן אָבֹת עַל־בָּנִים וְעַל־שִׁלֵּשִׁים וְעַל־רִבֵּעִים
לְשֹׂנְאָי: וְעֹשֶׂה חֶסֶד לַאֲלָפִים
לְאֹהֲבַי וּלְשֹׁמְרֵי מִצְוֹתָי: לֹא תִשָּׂא אֶת־שֵׁם־יְהוָֹה אֱלֹהֶיךָ
לַשָּׁוְא כִּי לֹא יְנַקֶּה יְהוָֹה אֵת אֲשֶׁר־יִשָּׂא אֶת־שְׁמוֹ לַשָּׁוְא:
שָׁמוֹר אֶת־יוֹם הַשַּׁבָּת לְקַדְּשׁוֹ
כַּאֲשֶׁר צִוְּךָ ׀ יְהוָֹה אֱלֹהֶיךָ שֵׁשֶׁת יָמִים
תַּעֲבֹד וְעָשִׂיתָ כָּל־מְלַאכְתֶּךָ וְיוֹם
הַשְּׁבִיעִי שַׁבָּת ׀ לַיהוָֹה אֱלֹהֶיךָ לֹא
תַעֲשֶׂה כָל־מְלָאכָה אַתָּה וּבִנְךָ־וּבִתֶּךָ וְעַבְדְּךָ־וַאֲמָתֶךָ וְשׁוֹרְךָ
וַחֲמֹרְךָ וְכָל־בְּהֶמְתֶּךָ וְגֵרְךָ אֲשֶׁר בִּשְׁעָרֶיךָ לְמַעַן יָנוּחַ עַבְדְּךָ וַאֲמָתְךָ
כָּמוֹךָ: וְזָכַרְתָּ כִּי־עֶבֶד הָיִיתָ ׀
בְּאֶרֶץ מִצְרַיִם וַיֹּצִאֲךָ יְהוָֹה אֱלֹהֶיךָ
מִשָּׁם בְּיָד חֲזָקָה וּבִזְרֹעַ נְטוּיָה
עַל־כֵּן צִוְּךָ יְהוָֹה אֱלֹהֶיךָ לַעֲשׂוֹת אֶת־יוֹם הַשַּׁבָּת:
כַּבֵּד אֶת־אָבִיךָ וְאֶת־אִמֶּךָ כַּאֲשֶׁר צִוְּךָ יְהוָֹה אֱלֹהֶיךָ
לְמַעַן ׀ יַאֲרִיכֻן יָמֶיךָ וּלְמַעַן יִיטַב לָךְ עַל הָאֲדָמָה אֲשֶׁר־יְהוָֹה אֱלֹהֶיךָ נֹתֵן לָךְ:
לֹא תִרְצָח וְלֹא תִנְאָף וְלֹא תִגְנֹב:
וְלֹא־תַעֲנֶה בְרֵעֲךָ עֵד שָׁוְא:
וְלֹא תַחְמֹד אֵשֶׁת רֵעֶךָ וְלֹא תִתְאַוֶּה בֵּית רֵעֶךָ
שָׂדֵהוּ וְעַבְדּוֹ וַאֲמָתוֹ שׁוֹרוֹ וַחֲמֹרוֹ וְכֹל אֲשֶׁר לְרֵעֶךָ:

בְּטַעַם הַתַּחְתּוֹן • Deut. 5:6–18

אָנֹכִי יְהוָֹה אֱלֹהֶיךָ אֲשֶׁר הוֹצֵאתִיךָ
מֵאֶרֶץ מִצְרַיִם מִבֵּית עֲבָדִים לֹא־
יִהְיֶה לְךָ אֱלֹהִים אֲחֵרִים עַל־
פָּנָי: לֹא־תַעֲשֶׂה לְךָ פֶסֶל כָּל־
תְּמוּנָה אֲשֶׁר בַּשָּׁמַיִם מִמַּעַל
וַאֲשֶׁר בָּאָרֶץ מִתַּחַת וַאֲשֶׁר בַּמַּיִם
מִתַּחַת לָאָרֶץ: לֹא־תִשְׁתַּחֲוֶה
לָהֶם וְלֹא תָעָבְדֵם כִּי אָנֹכִי יְהוָֹה
אֱלֹהֶיךָ אֵל קַנָּא פֹּקֵד עֲוֹן אָבוֹת עַל־בָּנִים וְעַל־שִׁלֵּשִׁים וְעַל־רִבֵּעִים
לְשֹׂנְאָי | וְעֹשֶׂה חֶסֶד לַאֲלָפִים
לְאֹהֲבַי וּלְשֹׁמְרֵי מִצְוֹתָי: לֹא תִשָּׂא אֶת־שֵׁם־יְהוָֹה אֱלֹהֶיךָ
לַשָּׁוְא כִּי לֹא יְנַקֶּה יְהוָֹה אֵת אֲשֶׁר־יִשָּׂא אֶת־שְׁמוֹ לַשָּׁוְא:
שָׁמוֹר אֶת־יוֹם הַשַּׁבָּת לְקַדְּשׁוֹ
כַּאֲשֶׁר צִוְּךָ ׀ יְהוָֹה אֱלֹהֶיךָ שֵׁשֶׁת יָמִים
תַּעֲבֹד וְעָשִׂיתָ כָּל־מְלַאכְתֶּךָ וְיוֹם
הַשְּׁבִיעִי שַׁבָּת ׀ לַיהוָֹה אֱלֹהֶיךָ לֹא
תַעֲשֶׂה כָל־מְלָאכָה אַתָּה וּבִנְךָ־וּבִתֶּךָ וְעַבְדְּךָ־וַאֲמָתֶךָ וְשׁוֹרְךָ
וַחֲמֹרְךָ וְכָל־בְּהֶמְתֶּךָ וְגֵרְךָ אֲשֶׁר בִּשְׁעָרֶיךָ לְמַעַן יָנוּחַ עַבְדְּךָ וַאֲמָתְךָ
כָּמוֹךָ: וְזָכַרְתָּ כִּי עֶבֶד הָיִיתָ ׀
בְּאֶרֶץ מִצְרַיִם וַיֹּצִאֲךָ יְהוָֹה אֱלֹהֶיךָ
מִשָּׁם בְּיָד חֲזָקָה וּבִזְרֹעַ נְטוּיָה
לָא תִרְצָח וְלֹא תִנְאָף וְלֹא תִגְנֹב:
וְלֹא־תַעֲנֶה בְרֵעֲךָ עֵד שָׁוְא:
וְלֹא־תַעֲנֶה בְרֵעֲךָ עֵד שָׁוְא:

Special Melodies

Special trope melodies are widely used in two other instances—for the concluding verse of each book of Torah and for the reading of the story of Creation on Simchat Torah.

The Conclusion of a Book of Torah

As each book of Torah is concluded, the congregation rises when the final words are chanted and responds with the words חֲזַק חֲזַק וְנִתְחַזֵּק (*Chazak chazak v'nitchazek*). In order to prepare for the congregation's chanting of these words, the concluding verse is sung in the following manner:

וַיִּישֶׂם בָּאָרוֹן בְּמִצְרָיִם: (חזק חזק ונתחזק)

לְעֵינֵי כָל־בֵּית־יִשְׂרָאֵל בְּכָל־מַסְעֵיהֶם: (חזק חזק ונתחזק)

בְּהַר סִינָי: (חזק חזק ונתחזק)

עַל יַרְדֵּן יְרֵחוֹ:   (חזק חזק ונתחזק)

לְעֵינֵי כָל־יִשְׂרָאֵל: (חזק חזק ונתחזק)

Simchat Torah

On Simchat Torah it is traditional in some communities for the reader to wait for the congregation before chanting the final words of each "day" and then conclude in the following manner:

וַיְהִי־עֶרֶב וַיְהִי־בֹקֶר יוֹם אֶחָד:

Here, for example, is the chant for the end of the second paragraph of the Book of Genesis:

וַיִּקְרָא אֱלֹהִים לָרָקִיעַ שָׁמָיִם   וַיְהִי־עֶרֶב וַיְהִי־בֹקֶר יוֹם שֵׁנִי:

In some communities the reader does not pause and wait for the congregation but simply proceeds without pause with the final words of each paragraph. Indeed, it is good to remember that many communities have developed their own traditions. There is no "right" or "wrong" way to chant Torah. On the contrary, these contrasting traditions are a wonderful reflection of the richness and diversity of Jewish tradition as it spans time and space.

Many other customs surround the reading of Torah. The Torah is divided into fifty-four weekly portions called פָּרָשׁוֹת (*parashot*) or סְדָרוֹת (*s'darot*). The title of each פָּרָשָׁה (*parashah*, singular) is usually, but not always, based upon its first important word. The third פָּרָשָׁה in the Book of Genesis, for example, is called *Lech-L'cha*. The final פָּרָשָׁה in Deuteronomy is called *V'zot Hab'rachah*. When each פָּרָשָׁה is chanted in the synagogue on Shabbat or weekdays, it, in turn, is divided into a number of sections. We call each of those sections an עֲלִיָה (*aliyah*; plural, עֲלִיּוֹת, *aliyot*).

How much of the פָּרָשָׁה is actually read in the synagogue on Shabbat? That depends on the congregation and its religious practices. In general, one of three practices is used:

1. In a traditional synagogue, the entire פָּרָשָׁה is read and is divided into עֲלִיּוֹת that are usually indicated in the *Chumash*. In such synagogues, there are always at least seven *aliyot* to the Torah on Shabbat morning, plus the מַפְטִיר (*maftir*).

2. Many synagogues read Torah according to the so-called Triennial Cycle, in which one-third of the פָּרָשָׁה is read each year. In such an arrangement, the first third of each פָּרָשָׁה would be read, for example, in the year 2000, the second third in 2001, the third third in 2002, until 2003 is reached, when the entire cycle begins again.

3. Many progressive synagogues abbreviate the reading, gearing the length of the *parashah* to their individual needs. The number of individuals called to the Torah may also vary. However, each עֲלִיָה should contain at least three verses.

The following is a list of the names of all the פָּרָשׁוֹת, as well as the chapters and verses contained within each פָּרָשָׁה.

Genesis

B'resheet	1:1-6:8
No-ach	6:9-11:32
Lech-L'cha	12:1-17:27
Vayera	18:1-22:24
Chayei Sarah	23:1-25:18
Tol'dot	25:19-28:9
Vayetze	28:10-32:3
Vayishlach	32:4-36:43
Vayeshev	37:1-40:23
Miketz	41:1-44:17
Vayigash	44:18-47:27
Vay'chi	47:28-50:26

Exodus

Sh'mot	1:1-6:1
Va-eira	6:2-9:35
Bo	10:1-13:16
B'shalach	13:17-17:16
Yitro	18:1-20:26
Mishpatim	21:1-24:18
T'rumah	25:11-27:19
T'tzaveh	27:20-30:10
Ki Tisa	30:11-34:35
Vayakhel	35:1-38:20
P'kudei	38:21-40:38

Leviticus

Vayikra	1:1-5:26
Tzav	6:1-8:36
Sh'mini	9:1-11:47
Tazri-a	12:1-13:59
M'tzora	14:1-15:33
Acharei Mot	16:1-18:30
K'doshim	19:1-20:27
Emor	21:1-24:23
B'har	25:1-26:2
B'chukotai	26:3-27:34

Numbers

B'midbar	1:1-4:20
Naso	4:21-7:89
B'ha-alot'cha	8:1-12:16
Sh'lach-L'cha	13:1-15:41
Korach	16:1-18:32
Chukat	19:1-22:1
Balak	22:2-25:9
Pinchas	25:10-30:1
Matot	30:2-32:42
Mas'ei	33:1-36:13

Deuteronomy

D'varim	1:1-3:22
Va-etchanan	3:32-7:11
Ekev	7:12-11:25
R'eh	11:26-16:17
Shof'tim	16:18-21:9
Ki Tetzei	21:10-25:19
Ki Tavo	26:1-29:8
Nitzavim	29:9-31:30
Vayelech	31:1-30
Ha-azinu	32:1-52
V'zot Hab'rachah	33:1-34:12

Special Sabbaths

Sh'kalim (Shabbat before Adar)	Weekly *Parashah* + Exodus 30:11-16
Zachor (Shabbat before Purim)	Weekly *Parashah* + Deuteronomy 25:1; 7-19
Parah (Shabbat before Hachodesh)	Weekly *Parashah* + Numbers 19:1-22
Hachodesh (Shabbat before Nisan)	Weekly *Parashah* + Exodus 12:1-20
Hagadol (Shabbat before Pesach)	Weekly *Parashah*
Rosh Chodesh (coinciding with Shabbat)	Weekly *Parashah* + Numbers 28:9-15
Machar Chodesh (day before Rosh Chodesh)	Weekly *Parashah*

High Holidays

First Day Rosh Hashanah	(Traditional) Genesis 21:1-34
	(Reform) Genesis 22:1-24
Second Day Rosh Hashanah	(Traditional) Genesis 22:1-24
	(Reform) Genesis 1:1-2:3
Shabbat Shuvah	Weekly *Parashah*
Yom Kippur Morning	(Traditional) Leviticus 16:1-34 + Numbers 29:7-11
	(Reform) Deuteronomy 29:9-14; 30:11-20
Yom Kippur Afternoon	(Traditional) Leviticus 18:1-30
	(Reform) Leviticus 19:1-4; 9-18; 32-37

Festivals: Sukot, Pesach, Shavuot

Sukot First Day	Leviticus 22:26-23:24
Sukot Second Day	Same as above
Shabbat during Sukot	Exodus 33:12-34:26
Eighth Day (Sh'mini Atzeret)	Deuteronomy 14:22-16:17
Simchat Torah	Deuteronomy 33:1 to the end of Torah + Genesis 1:1-2:3
Pesach First Day	Exodus 12:21-51
Pesach Second Day	Leviticus 22:26-23:44
Shabbat during Pesach	Exodus 33:12-34:26
Pesach Seventh Day	Exodus 13:17-15:26
Pesach Eighth Day	Deuteronomy 15:19-16:17

Shavuot First Day   Exodus 19:1-20:23
Shavuot Second Day   Deuteronomy 15:19-16:17

Other Days

Tishah B'av Morning   Deuteronomy 4:30-40
Tishah B'av Afternoon   Exodus 32:11-14; 34:1-10
Public Fasts   All readings as on Tishah B'av
Shabbat during Chanukah   Weekly *Parashah*
Second Shabbat Chanukah   Weekly *Parashah*
Purim   Exodus 17:8-16
Yom HaSho-ah   Deuteronomy 4:30-40
Yom Ha-Atzma-ut   Deuteronomy 11:8-21

The trope you have learned in this book is Torah trope for Shabbat and weekdays. There is one time during the year that we use a different version of Torah trope and that is during the High Holy Days. On the mornings of Rosh Hashanah and Yom Kippur, High Holy Day cantillation is used for the readings from Genesis and Deuteronomy. (According to tradition, Shabbat trope is used on Yom Kippur afternoon.) This trope functions exactly in the same way as the one you have learned, i.e., it has the same clauses with *m'chabrim* and *mafsikim*. However, the melodies of the *ta-amei hamikra* are different. In the back of this book, you will find the musical notation for the High Holy Day trope. Below are the most common trope clauses and patterns chanted in High Holy Day cantillation.

מֵרְכָא טִפְחָא מֻנַּח אֶתְנַחְתָּא   **84**

מֵרְכָא טִפְחָא מֵרְכָא סוֹף־פָּסוּק:

קַדְמָא מַהְפַּךְ פַּשְׁטָא מֻנַּח קָטֹן

זָקֵף גָּדוֹל

יְתִיב מֻנַּח קָטֹן

קַדְמָא דַּרְגָּא תְּבִיר

קַדְמָא מֵרְכָא תְּבִיר

מֻנַּח ׀ מֻנַּח רְבִיעִי

קַדְמָא וְאַזְלָא

גֵּרְשַׁיִם

תְּלִישָׁא־קְטַנָּה

פָּזֵר

תְּלִישָׁא גְדוֹלָה

מֻנַּח זַרְקָא מֻנַּח סֶגוֹל

(final cadence): מֵרְכָא טִפְחָא מֵרְכָא סוֹף־פָּסוּק

One of the most helpful tools for a Torah reader is a *tikkun*, also called *tikkun korim* or *sefer tikkun*. The word *tikkun* is deeply embedded in Judaism and has many different connotations. For our purposes, a *tikkun* (coming from the Hebrew word "to repair," as in the familiar phrase *tikkun olam*, "repairing the world") is a book that presents the vocalized Hebrew of the Pentateuch side by side with the unvocalized calligraphy you will see in the Torah scroll. You can find a good *tikkun*—there are now many to choose from—in your Hebrew bookstore. As you leaf through it, you will notice some interesting things.

In many editions of the *tikkun*, letters are used to indicate verse and chapter numbers. In Hebrew, each letter of the alphabet is assigned a numerical value: Thus verse 18 is notated as יח. A complete list of all the letters and their numerical values appears on the next page for easy reference.

The unvocalized side of the *tikkun* is clearly divided into paragraphs, and these divisions denote exactly the way the Torah scroll is written. In some cases, the blank space continues through the end of the line, and the text continues at the margin on the next line (for example, Genesis 1:5 going to Genesis 1:6). This is called a *p'tuchah* (open section), and the "shorthand" symbol for this in a standard *Chumash* is simply the letter פ. In contrast to the *p'tuchah* is the *s'tumah*, in which there is open space after some text but then new text continues on the same line. You will find an example of *s'tumah* between chapters 1 and 2 of the Book of Genesis. A standard *Chumash* indicates this interruption with the letter ס.

In addition, there are footnotes in the *tikkun* that are often important to the reader, sometimes telling the reader to read a word differently from the way it appears in the scroll (*k'ri uch'tiv*) or to chant the word in a particular way. This may be because the word is too earthy to be read in public and a euphemism is substituted (as in Deuteronomy 28:30), or there may actually be a grammatical or spelling error in the text (as in Exodus 39:4). If your Hebrew isn't quite up to deciphering these footnotes, consult an authority with expertise in the *Masorah*, which is the edited Torah that has come down to us today.

On the following page you will find an annotated example of a page from a *tikkun*.

Hebrew Numeral Table

1	א
2	בּ ב
3	ג
4	ד
5	ה
6	ו
7	ז
8	ח
9	ט
10	י
20	כּ כ ך
30	ל
40	מ ם
50	נ ן
60	ס
70	ע
80	פּ פ ף
90	צ ץ
100	ק
200	ר
300	שׁ שׂ
400	ת

Hebrew name of the portion: B'resheet

On this page you find (parts of) chapters 3 and 4.

Hebrew name of the Book of Genesis

These letters indicate the beginning of verse 17.

בראשית

ג - ד

בראשית

Beginning of the (traditional) fourth aliyah

S'tumah ("closed") paragraph

Beginning of chapter 4, verse 1.

P'tucha ("open") paragraph

Some letters are embellished with "crowns". This does not change the pronunciation or the chant.

GLOSSARY OF TERMS RELATED TO THE RITUAL OF READING TORAH

- *Aliyah*: (plural, *aliyot*) Literally, "ascent." The honor extended to a congregant whereby she or he is called up to the reading of the Torah. The following is the traditional number of *aliyot* for reading the Torah:

    - **Weekdays** (Monday and Thursday): Three *aliyot*.

    - **Rosh Chodesh (New Month)**: Four on a weekday; seven plus *maftir* on Shabbat.

    - **Fast Days**: Three at morning service; three at afternoon service (the third is *maftir*).

    - **Rosh Hashanah**: Five plus *maftir* on a weekday; seven plus *maftir* on Shabbat.

    - **Yom Kippur**: Six plus *maftir* on a weekday; seven plus *maftir* on Shabbat; three (the third is *maftir*) at afternoon service.

    - **Three Festivals (Pesach, Shavuot, Sukot)**: Five plus *maftir* on a weekday; seven plus *maftir* on Shabbat.

    - **Shabbat**: Seven plus *maftir*.

- *Amen*: Literally, "so be it." The response recited after hearing a blessing.

- *Aron Hakodesh*: The Holy Ark, which is used to house the Torah scrolls.

- *Atzei Chayim* (singular, *etz chayim*): Literally, trees of life. The wooden handles of the Torah.

- *Aufruf*: From the Yiddish "to call up." Calling up of the bride and groom to the Torah for an *aliyah* on the Shabbat before their wedding.

- *Avnet*: The belt that holds the Torah scroll, which is closed when the Torah is not in use.

- *Ba-al/Ba-alat Koreh* (also *Ba-al/Ba-alat K'ree-ah*): The individual who reads aloud from the Torah for the congregation.

- *Bimah*: The pulpit or reader's desk.

- *Birkat Hagomel*: A special benediction recited during the Torah service by anyone who has escaped a serious danger, such as illness, accident, etc.

- *Chazak, chazak, v'nitchazek*: "From strength to strength, let us strengthen one another." At the end of each *sefer* in the Torah are blank lines. When the reader reaches that point, she or he should stop and allow the congregation to chant the words *Chazak, chazak, v'nitchazek.* Then the reader repeats, *Chazak, chazak, v'nitchazek.*

- **Chumash**: Literally, "Fifth." The first five books of the Bible, referred to as the Five Books of Moses. Pentateuch is the Greek term for *Chumash.*

- **Dikduk**: Hebrew/biblical grammar.

- **Gabai**: The synagogue functionary who assists during the public reading of Torah.

- **G'lilah**: The tying/dressing of the Torah scroll.

- **Golel** (m.)/**golelet** (f.): The person who ties the Torah scroll and dresses it after the reading.

- **Haftarah**: The reading from the Prophets that follows Shabbat and holiday Torah readings.

- **Hagba-ah**: The raising of the Torah at the conclusion of the reading.

- **Hakafah** (plural, *hakafot*): The processional through the synagogue with the Torah scroll before and/or after the Torah reading.

- **Keter Torah**: The crownlike ornament that is placed atop the Torah scroll (different from *rimonim*).

- **K'ri-at HaTorah**: The public reading of Torah in the synagogue.

- **K'ri uch'tiv**: Literally, "read and written." An instance in which a word is read from the Torah differently from the way it is written.

- **Mafsik** (plural, *mafsikim*): The general name for a cantillation mark that functions as a separator.

- **Maftir**: Both the last *aliyah* and the last person to be called up to the reading of Torah. Often that person also reads the *haftarah.*

- **Magbiah**(m.)/**Magbihah**(f.): The person who is called up to raise the Torah scroll in front of the congregation at the conclusion of the reading.

- **M'chaber** (plural, *m'chabrim*): The general name for a cantillation mark that functions as a connector.

- **M'il**: The Torah mantle.

- **Meteg**: Accent mark used to indicate secondary accents in Torah.

- **Minhag**: Custom.

- *Minhag Hamakom*: Literally, the "custom of the place." The term for following the custom of the community in which a person is praying.

- *Ner Tamid*: The Eternal Light.

- *Parashah* (plural, *parashiyot* or *parashot*): A "section or part." The specific section of Torah assigned for reading in the synagogue each week and on each festival, fast, and Holy Day.

- *Parashat Hashavu-a*: The Torah portion of the week.

- *Pasuk*: A verse or sentence.

- *Pasul*: Ritually unfit.

- *Pentateuch*: See *Chumash*.

- *Perek* (plural, *p'rakim*): Chapter.

- *P'sik*: A vertical line between two words indicating a short pause. Exception: When a *p'sik* is found between two *munachim* and is then followed by *r'vi-i*, the *p'sik* is a part of *munach l'garmeih*.

- *P'tuchah*: Literally, "opening." The open space at the end of a *pasuk* in the *Sefer Torah*, indicated in the *Chumash* by the letter פ.

- *Rimonim* (singular, *rimon*): "Pomegranates." Ornaments that adorn each wooden pole of the wrapped Torah scroll.

- *Sidrah*: The weekly portion of the Torah, used interchangeably with *parashah*.

- *Sefer* (plural, *s'farim*): Book.

- *Sefer Torah* (plural, *Sifrei Torah*): The actual Torah scroll used during worship, as opposed to a printed *Chumash*.

- *S'tumah* (also *s'gurah*): Literally, "closed." The closed space at the end of a *pasuk* in the *Sefer Torah*, indicated by the letter ס.

- *Ta-am* (plural, *t'amim*): Literally, "taste" or "sense," also "accent." A cantillation mark or symbol.

- *Ta-amei Hamikra*: Cantillation symbols.

- *Trope*: Cantillation, from the Greek word *tropos*, meaning "style" or "way."

- *Yad*: Literally, "hand." The pointer used by a Torah reader.

21. גֵּרֵשׁ

22. גֵּרְשַׁיִּם

23. יְתִיב מֻנַּח קָטֹן

24. יְתִיב קָטֹן

25. זָקֵף גָּדֹוֹל

26. מֻנַּח זַרְקָא מֻנַּח סֶגוֹל

27. זַרְקָא מֻנַּח סֶגוֹל

28. מֻנַּח זַרְקָא סֶגוֹל

29. זַרְקָא סֶגוֹל

30. מֵרְכָא טִפְחָא מֵרְכָא סוֹף־פָּסֽוּק:

31. מֵרְכָא טִפְחָא סוֹף־פָּסֽוּק:

32. טִפְחָא מֵרְכָא סוֹף־פָּסֽוּק:

33. טִפְחָא סוֹף־פָּסֽוּק:

Avenary, Hanoch. *The Ashkenazic Tradition of Biblical Chant Between 1500 and 1900.* Tel Aviv: Tel Aviv University Press, 1978.

Binder, A. W. *Biblical Chant.* New York: Philosophical Library, 1959.

Encyclopedia Judaica. "Cantillation," "Masoretic Accents," "Masorah." Jerusalem: Keter Publishing House, 1972.

Idelsohn, A. Z. *Jewish Music in Its Historical Development.* Westport: Greenwood Press, 1981.

Kadari, Y'hudah. *V'shinantam L'vanecha.* Jerusalem: R'nanot, Hamachon L'muzikah Y'hudit, 1994.

Leneman, Helen. *Bar/Bat Mitzvah Education.* Denver: A. R. E. Publishing, Inc., 1993.

Rosenbaum, Samuel. *A Guide to Haftarah Chanting.* Hoboken: Ktav Publishing House, 1973.

Rosenberg, Yitzchok Mordechai. *T'aamim L'korim.* New York: Chadish Press, 1980.

Rosowsky, Solomon. *Cantillation of the Bible.* New York: Reconstructionist Press, 1957.

Schleifer, Dr. Eliyahu. "*Cantillation*" from Encyclopedia of Judaism. Jerusalem, 1989.

Shiloah, Amnon. *Jewish Musical Traditions.* Detroit: Wayne State University Press, 1992.

Simon, Dr. Ely. *The Complete Torah Reading Handbook.* Brooklyn: The Judaica Press, Inc., 1996.

Spiro, Pinchas. *Haftarah Chanting.* New York: Board of Jewish Education, 1978.

_____. *Teachers' Guide to Haftarah Chanting.* New York: Cantors Assembly, 1995.

Werner, Eric. *A Voice Still Heard.* University Park: Pennsylvania State University Press, 1976.